Isle Royale National Park

EAGLE HARBOR
COPPER HARBOR
CALUMET
HANCOCK   HUBBELL
HOUGHTON   LAKE LINDEN
CHASSELL   JACOBSVILLE
NAGON
GREENLAND
BARAGA   L'ANSE   BIG BAY
NEGAUNEE
ALBERTA
ISHPEMING   CHRISTMAS
MARQUETTE
AU TRAIN
MUNISING

Pictured Rocks
Nat. Lakeshore
GRAND MARAIS

WHITEFISH POINT
PARADISE

NAUBINWAY
MANISTIQUE
GULLIVER
GLADSTONE
ESCANABA

SAULT STE. MARIE   Sugar Island
Neebish Island
CEDARVILLE
ST. IGNACE
EPOUFETTE   HESSEL   Drummond Island
GROS CAP   DETOUR VILLAGE
Mackinac Bridge
Mackinac Island
Bois Blanc Island
CHEBOYGAN

Beaver Island   CROSS VILLAGE
MENOMINEE
HARBOR SPRINGS
MACKINAW CITY
ROGERS CITY

NORTHPORT
LELAND
Manitou Islands
PETOSKY
CHARLEVOIX
PESHAWBESTOWN
ALPENA

GLEN HAVEN
Sleeping Bear Dunes National Lakeshore
SUTTONS BAY
KEWADIN
ELK RAPIDS
HARRISVILLE

FRANKFORT
EMPIRE
TRAVERSE CITY
Interlochen National Music Camp
ELBERTA
ARCADIA
OSCODA
AU SABLE
TAWAS CITY

MANISTEE

PORT AUSTIN
GRINDSTONE CITY
PORT HOPE
OMER
STANDISH
PINCONNING
CASEVILLE
BAY PORT
SEBEWAING
HARBOR BEACH

LUDINGTON
PENTWATER
BAY CITY   ESSEXVILLE
PORT SANILAC

WHITEHALL-MONTAGUE
MUSKEGON
GRAND HAVEN
LEXINGTON

HOLLAND
DOUGLAS-SAUGATUCK
PORT HURON
ST. CLAIR
MARINE CITY
ALGONAC
MOUNT CLEMENS
ST. CLAIR SHORES
DETROIT
ECORSE
WYANDOTTE
TRENTON
GROSSE ISLE
Harsen's Island
WINDSOR

SOUTH HAVEN

BENTON HARBOR-ST. JOSEPH
BRIDGMAN
GRAND BEACH
MICHIANA   NEW BUFFALO
MONROE

TOLEDO

THE
LONG BLUE EDGE
OF
SUMMER

A VACATION GUIDE TO THE SHORELINES
OF MICHIGAN

BY DORIS SCHARFENBERG

WILLIAM B. EERDMANS PUBLISHING COMPANY

To
JIM
BRUCE
DOUGLAS
JANE
GRETCHEN

Copyright © 1982 by Wm. B. Eerdmans Publishing Company
255 Jefferson Ave., S.E., Grand Rapids, MI 49503

Reprinted, April 1983

Library of Congress Cataloging in Publication Data

Scharfenberg, Doris, 1925-
The long blue edge of summer.
1. Michigan—Description and travel—1981   —Guide-
books. 2. Great Lakes region—Description and travel—
Guide-books. 3. Outdoor recreation—Michigan—Guide-
books. I. Title.
F564.3.S3   917.74'0443   81-19621
ISBN 0-8028-7044-9   AACR2

CONTENTS

FEATURE ARTICLES

ACKNOWLEDGMENTS

The author and publisher wish to acknowledge the contributions of those who helped in the production of this book:

Michigan Travel Bureau for the photo on page 204; all other photos are the author's;

Michigan State University Press and Robert Brent for illustrations from the *Atlas of Michigan,* copyright © 1977 by Michigan State University Press;

Louise Bauer for the maps;

Joel Beversluis for the design and layout;

Sandra Nowlin for editorial supervision.

PREFACE

I was Detroit's own kid. Mother was one of the city's earliest policewomen and father ran a home insulation business; vacationing did not loom large in their busy lives. Trips to Belle Isle, the zoo, swimming and hiking at Rouge Park, and streetcar rides downtown to meet my mother filled our summer.

Once in a while, however, there was a magnificent moment when my brother and I were piled into the car and in a mood of intense merriment the family drove to the shores of Lake Huron or Lake Michigan to spend the night at a tourist home some place where we could see one of the big lakes.

The sight of that water has never ceased to thrill me. Away from the obscuring trees and close walls of tight-packed houses, away from the deep canyons of mid-town commerce, the sight of nothing but clear distant space was intoxicating. Shining gray or dazzling blue, depending on the mood of the sky . . . a world exquisite in its emptiness yet magically full when you really looked. For me the water's fresh-blown scents were better than cookies in the oven or lilacs in full bloom. I loved every split second of being near that long blue edge.

When marriage came, followed by four children, our life-pattern was different—but the goal the same. I took them to the shores as naturally as a duck leads her hatchlings to the pond. But where my experience had been confined to flashing moments as limited as an afternoon of theater, they had gifts of time plus well-advanced recreational facilities.

Michigan state parks (thirty-eight of them along the shore) lead the nation in marked trails, modern equipment, and sheer numbers. Three national forests, six state forests, and two national lakeshores provide thousands of quiet havens where families or the solitary wanderer can kick the surf, wake up to nonaerosol pine scents, and change pace.

The State Waterways Commission has developed a string of sixty-five protective harbors, insuring that no boater will be more than fifteen miles away from shoreline safety. As never before the merry sound of summer festivals rings around the lakes. New attention is being paid to historic sites; new sports (hang gliding, sail surfing) are thriving. Fishing, as always, is phenomenally popular.

There *are* problems, though. Our children's children will have to make reservations for tent space or docking privileges even though the number of public and private campgrounds and marinas has enormously increased. Vacations can no longer be the impulse-triggered happenings they once were, but will require looking ahead a bit.

Go slow, explore, enjoy each region. If Michigan's 3,000 miles of shoreline were suddenly twisted into a rope it would reach from New York to San Francisco and dangle in both oceans. You *could* do it all in one summer, and maybe make it into a book of records ... à la Guinness. One section at a time is better.

I have concentrated on parks, points of interest, scenic views, and the like, and left unmentioned many fine private resorts and hotels facing the water. The Automobile Club of Michigan and other guides do a better job than I could possibly do in rating and recommending restaurants and motels, so (with rare exceptions) I have skipped these matters.

In general (also with rare exceptions) all attractions listed are on the waterfront, less than five miles from shore, or are an integral part of the locale. Greenfield Village or the National Music Camp at Interlochen, for example, *had* to be included.

Costs and hours are a real headache. One way to cut costs is to shorten hours; one way to stay in business is to raise fees. What is true as the book is written may be inaccurate by the time it is purchased. Therefore, I haven't said much about prices that are under three dollars; fees quoted over that are subject to change but may allow you to estimate.

My thanks to the many people who helped check out the data, and to the folks along the shores who answered my questions. I greatly appreciated the advice and encouragement of the Detroit Women Writers, of Bettie Cannon, Iris Jones, Marilyn Lyman, and others. Cheers also to Marcia Danner, Len Barnes, Bob Helwig, John Maters, Robert Wenkam, and Jim Vesely, to the staff of Michigan's Travel Bureau, and to my patient family.

Our coast is a wonder, a garland of beach and rock unmatched anywhere on the planet. Go with sensitivity to that azure world; awareness of other's rights and environmental protection is not only a matter of civilized behavior but of survival. Love and care for each area; after all, *you* own it. Country-born or city kid, in Michigan we are *very* rich.

DORIS SCHARFENBERG

Along Lake Erie

PART ONE

TOLEDO TO PORT HURON

LAKE ERIE; THE DETROIT RIVER; DETROIT; LAKE ST. CLAIR AND THE ST. CLAIR RIVER

PORT HURON
ST. CLAIR
MARINE CITY
ALGONAC
MOUNT CLEMENS
ST. CLAIR SHORES
DETROIT
ECORSE
WYANDOTTE
TRENTON
GROSSE ISLE
MONROE
TOLEDO
Harsen's Island
WINDSOR

LAKE ERIE STATISTICS

Length	241 miles
Width	57 miles
Length of coastline including Canada and islands	871 miles
Total water surface	9,910 square miles
United States water surface	4,980 square miles
Total land drainage basin	22,700 square miles
United States drainage	18,000 square miles
Maximum depth	210 feet
Average depth	62 feet
Volume of water	116 cubic miles

LAKE ERIE

I is easy to suppose that Lake Erie was named by a homesick Irishman, but that isn't the case. The word is thought to be Iroquois for "cat," referring perhaps to the large number of wildcats stalking the tall shore grasses or to the nearby tribes declared by the Iroquois to look like cats.

The name fits. Like a traditional tabby, Lake Erie is an independent, inscrutable creation; moody, fickle, and yet full of play. The shallowest of the Great Lakes (average depth is less than sixty feet), its long grey and glassy surface can raise a hackle of waves in minutes and leap over the breakwaters with alarming agility. Experienced boaters know this as a dangerous body of water.

Erie was the last of the big lakes to be discovered and settled by incoming Europeans. Voyageurs paddling their canoes up the St. Lawrence were stopped by that spectacular navigational block called Niagara Falls, so they stroked and portaged toward Georgian Bay and upper lakes regions first. Besides, it was in a northwest direction that treasured beaver skins were most plentiful and where a shortcut to the wealth of China was rumored to be waiting.

French missionaries in the mid-1600s, soon followed by trappers and traders, put together a clump of crude cabins along the banks of the Raisin River, initiating the development of Monroe County. This rough little community, just a few canoe-lengths from where the Raisin opened into Lake Erie, saw the first American flag flown in Michigan territory and grew up to be the city of Monroe.

In territorial days Michiganians thought their share of the Erie coast ought to include the mouth of the Maumee River plus Toledo, and the resulting squabble with Ohio nearly became a real war. Ohio's great advantage was heavier clout in Congress, having achieved statehood some years earlier. Washington settled the dispute by giving Toledo to the Buckeyes and bestowing upon Michigan the western half of the Upper Peninsula, a decision not accepted in good grace until it became clear that the mineral-rich U.P. was a bonanza addition.

Official state road maps show the stretch of coast along Lake Erie to be a fairly smooth line. You'll find, however, that it is actually an irregular squiggle with half-a-dozen creek and river outlets and endless numbers of dead-end roads. There is no path straight along the waterfront and the seeker of access sites can easily get lost behind solid walls of cottages that have closed their flanks to invaders. (This situation holds quite true for the next 3,000 miles!)

Folks traveling north on I-75 from Ohio will see nothing of the lake. Between the expressway and the coast is a lot of wide, flat, and often soggy land, much of it state property open to summer anglers and fall duck hunters. The meandering patterns of marsh and open lagoons are popular with bird watchers tracking migratory waterfowl or photographing the ballets of mass flight.

In late July and most of August, blooming lotus blossoms cover acres of water, much as they do in Louisiana's bayous. The "shining lilies" are said to have been planted by Indians from the south who called them "chestnuts of the waters" and savored the nutlike roots.

Perch is the biggest catch hereabouts, but those who propose to fish will be happy to know that walleyes are back in full quantity now that Lake Erie has been rescued from the death-grip of pollution. Crappie and catfish are also high on the list. (Crappies move in schools ten to twenty feet deep. If you catch one, anchor and keep fishing!)

The long blue edge begins at the state line, a boundary shared with the northern city limits of Toledo.

Take the Summit Street exit off I-75, turn east, then east again on
Algonquin Street for a short-short drive to site. Minimum facilities,
no water tap. Leads out into the lake via North Maumee Bay.

● HALFWAY
 CREEK
 ACCESS SITE

E. Sterns and Summit Street. Under the direction of several government agencies, a favored spot for nonboaters; with parking
space—but that's about all. Open to fall hunting.

● ERIE SHOREFISHING
 SITE

Follow the Erie Road exit off I-75 east past the Consumer's Power
Company plant (those tall twin smokestacks) to a small, unimproved parking area on the edge of the lake. No facilities, only
trash barrels, but a long nice hike through a thin, grassy snippet
of land.

● WOODTICK
 PENINSULA PARK

Exit off I-75 east at Luna Pier. The name conjures visions of a
walkway into Lake Erie, but all you'll find is a small park with a
platform on a dike for boatwatchers. No walking along this rough
barricade and only a tiny spot of open public beach. Luna has no
pier.

● LUNA PIER

A primitive access site on the north side of Otter Creek, but don't
try to find it without a county map. Too complicated for the value
received to give directions here; just wanted you to know of its
existence. Shore fishing along the creek, very small launching area
for canoes. The short pier into Lake Erie is unusable.

● OTTER CREEK

Between Otter Creek Road and La Plaisance on north-bound I-75.

● TRAVEL INFORMATION

Take La Plaisance Road exit east to Harbor Road. With parking
space for fifty cars, pit toilets, and a pier, this is a popular launching
site for all trailerable boats. At the mouth of La Plaisance Creek
and still under development.

● HOFFMAN
 MEMORIAL ACCESS
 SITE

   In the *Michigan Harbors Guide* the spot is listed as Bolles
Harbor. For incoming small craft, there are ten transient accommodations (as of this writing), gasoline, haul-out facilities, restrooms, and so forth at the Monroe Boat Club a few hundred feet
upstream.

5

MONROE HARBOR • The mouth of the Raisin River has some private boat docking spots and you can sail small craft upstream (i.e., uptown) to the Hellenberg Field Access Site with a hard ramp and parking for fifty cars. Off Front Street, east of railroad bridge, south side of the river.

MONROE • Canopies of wild grapes covered the trees and bushes along the banks of the river first settled by the French. Quite naturally they dubbed it the "Riviere aux Raisins."

During the War of 1812 the title was more than a name; it became a national battle cry. In the years after the American Revolution when nobody was really sure who owned what, the British-Canadian authorities tried to make the River Raisin the international boundary line. That would keep the Great Lakes neatly in British territory.

However, the Americans wanted the lakes, also. It was just too much when a tough Indian leader called Tecumseh led his braves in a massacre of incoming settlers and Kentucky soldiers (who had been taken prisoner and promised safety by the British). The whole country shouted "Remember the Raisin" and vowed to fight. In short order the river and its community were recaptured by Americans, once and for all becoming American land ... with the British pushed to the far shores of the big dividing waters.

Monroe is heritage-conscious, takes care of its vintage houses, and supports an active Historical Society. Former Governor McClelland's home and the Ilgenfritz House on Elm Street are in the National Register of Historic Sites.

A name that looms large in Monroe is that of controversial General George C. Custer, he of the "last stand." Born in Ohio, Custer went to school in Monroe for a time and later came back to marry the girl he just couldn't forget ... who followed him to other regions. Not quite a true native son, he is nonetheless honored as one via a mighty statue of him and his horse on the corner of North Monroe and Elm; and the name "Custer" is in abundance around town.

A sleek new city hall and classical late Victorian courthouse are close to an old home serving as the Monroe Public Library. An historic marker designating the site of an early whipping post—seldom used—is across the street.

Today Monroe has a population of 24,000, plenty of parks, playgrounds, and totlots, plus a couple of golf courses. In the summer months the County Library presents free Monday-night movies on Loranger Square in downtown Monroe. Pick up a schedule and it might be your luck to watch Laurel and Hardy under the stars.

The Monroe County Historical Museum, 126 S. Monroe, dotes on Custer memorabilia, and would like to show you its Indian treasures, pans, and pottery of the past. Museum hours (summer only): Tues.-Sun., 10:00 AM to 5:00 PM.

Summer funfare includes the Floral City Festival and Old Frenchtown Day, both in July, and the Monroe County Fair in August. For exact dates and more information, contact the Monroe County Chamber of Commerce, 22 W. Second Street, Monroe, Michigan 48161. 313/242-3366.

North Dixie Highway and State Park Road. Further proof of improved Lake Erie water conditions is the fact that swimming has returned to the only state park along its shore. There are nearly a thousand acres of picnic and boating opportunities at Sterling; 192 campsites offer electricity, flush toilets, and sanitation station, but no park naturalist. Nature museum, bridle and hiking trails, and daytime refreshment stand. 313/289-2715.

● STERLING STATE PARK

A familiar coastal landmark, the twin cooling towers of the center will let groups of six to fifty persons come and get a closer look. There's a slide show, models, and displays and the tour is recommended for ages fourteen through adult. Reservations are absolutely essential since staff guides are not always available. If you get the come-ahead, use Dixie Highway to E. Fermi Drive. Contact the plant at Newport, Michigan 48166. 313/586-2362.

● ENRICO FERMI II ENERGY INFORMATION CENTER (ATOMIC POWER PLANT)

No public facilities in this cottage community.

● ESTRAL BEACH

Limited parking space and launching for small boats only. Dixie Highway and Swan Creek Road.

● SWAN CREEK ACCESS SITE

7

POINTE MOUILEE ● Southeast of South Rockwood off Roberts Road and U.S. Turnpike
STATE GAME AREA (which turns into Jefferson further north). Large waterfront reserve with primitive facilities, no camping, etc. It includes the last large bays before the Detroit River and also takes in both sides of the mouth of the Huron River. Hunting in season; good perch and walleye fishing out in the lake. Department of Natural Resources, 313/379-9692.

From this point the population increases a thousandfold and the next stretch of water is a far different story.

THE DETROIT RIVER

I T *looks* like a river, we call it a river, but the narrow channel between Lakes St. Clair and Erie is a *straits*, a downspout draining the contents of our sweet seas into still another basin.

In a short thirty-two-mile run the river (semantic technicalities aside) rushes, whirls, and eddies past the "seven Sisters" smokestacks of Detroit Edison, past the bobbing poles of hopeful anglers on Belle Isle, the gray glass towers of Detroit and its Canadian cousin, Windsor, Ontario. . . .

Its waters slap against the steel sanctuaries of vast industrial complexes full of salt piles, coal piles, giant chimneys, great loading devices, docked freighters, rail yards, and structures that strangely resemble black hen houses enlarged to an irrational size.

Straight across from such mega-biz, the water that has journeyed from Lake Superior soaks into the deep reaches of a wetlands area where tall grass and splashing space are just what a nesting duck needs.

Quiet homesites face the river's rippling reflections; parks and walkways frequent its banks. Overhead a steady stream of cars across the Ambassador Bridge vouches for the friendliness of the border. Beneath the current lies the world's first international vehicular tunnel.

Few waterways can claim such variety in so short a span, nor is there a river equal in traffic. More cargo tonnage and more pleasure boats use the Detroit River than the Thames, Seine, Volga, and Rhine—for all their length—combined.

Three centuries back, during the Old World's seesaw struggle for power on the new continent, a Frenchman, Antoine de la Mothe Cadillac, suggested that a settlement built along *Le Detroit* (the straits) would be a smart strategic move against the ambitions of the English. He took leave of his post as Commandant of Fort de Buade at St. Ignace and came with a whole navy of canoes to find the right spot.

It wasn't too hard a choice. Land near Lake Erie was just a swamp, and other sites lacked protection. On July 24, 1701, Monsieur Cadillac climbed up a high section of river bank with a clear view upstream and downstream and gave his nod of approval. Within hours logs were being felled for a fort; Cadillac had opened the Detroit River's first recorded chapter.

In the twisting course of history the growing settlement went from French to British to American hands. Canoes gave way to sails and steam, and the riverfront farms were pushed back for industry. It wasn't long before the area population touched both lakes, and fiefdoms of private enterprise—Ford's River Rouge, Wyandotte Chemicals, and others—eventually rose over the regions Cadillac saw as useless bog.

The Detroit River's role as international boundary line could give peace lessons to the embattled borders of the world, but there *have* been troubles. Long after the War of 1812, American feeling ran high that the British-Canadians would try again, coming over the river because it was the narrowest point. Fort Wayne (very well preserved but nearly hidden by surrounding buildings) was built with that sneaky possibility in mind. Guns were mounted but a shot was never fired; the lookouts reported no advancing boats and eventually the increasing commerce between the would-be enemies became more important than hostility.

During the years before the Civil War the Detroit River was the last barrier between a runaway slave and freedom in Canada via the "underground railroad." In later times traffic of a less noble purpose thrived when the river gave a sporting challenge to Prohibition rum runners, and a headache to authorities.

Pollution and control of heavy congestion are the biggest prob-

lems today. The Coast Guard keeps watch, gives boat-handling courses, and so forth, but 900-foot freighters, sailboats, speed-boats, and what-have-yous using the same short stretch of water is clearly hazardous to a sailor's health.

Long ore carriers move like silent visions where the canoes of the Hurons, voyageurs, and settlers once passed. History described as a flowing river remains a fresh cliché.

Gibralter, Trenton, Wyandotte, Ecorse, and River Rouge are all part of the greater Detroit metropolitan area known as the down-river communities, and all have personalities of their own plus an exceptional share of heavy industry. It has been a struggle for them to keep any of their waterfront property open to the public although there are some surprisingly pleasant spots.

● TRENTON

The Elizabeth Park Marina and Launching Site entrances face the Grosse Isle Parkway. Will take all trailerable boats, and has rest-room facilities in a lovely tree-filled park setting.

In mid-town (by now U.S. Turnpike has turned into Jefferson; it will also become Biddle—all the same street) there's a nice park with an all-purpose launching site plus a couple of "porches" with benches for ship watchers. Launchers must get permit from police department.

● RIVERVIEW

Boat ramp for residents only. No park or pier.

● GROSSE ISLE

There are no public facilities on Grosse Isle, but it is an exceed-ingly pleasant place to go for a drive. Lovely homes and a very good ice-cream parlor in the shopping district toward the east side.

● WYANDOTTE

Between the enormous silhouettes of the Wyandotte Chemical Company and other giants, the city has a park on Van Alstyne, one block east of Biddle. The *Harbors Guide* lists mooring facilities for a few transient boats; the rest are for residents. Restrooms, water, telephone, and so forth, and a local stop for the Bob-Lo boat.

11

One block from the waterfront on Biddle Avenue two marvelous old mansions face each other like a pair of retired dowager queens. One is the Wyandotte Public Library, the other (the big white one) is the "new" home of the Wyandotte Historical Museum, open three days a week: Tues. 10:00–4:00, Thurs. 12:00–4:00, Sun. 2:00–5:00. 2610 Biddle, Wyandotte, Michigan 48192. 313/283-0818.

Ethnic festivals head the weekend programs at Yack Arena, Maple and 3rd Streets. Call Taylor Chamber of Commerce, 313/284-6000.

Privately operated boat launching is available on the Ecorse (north) end of town, just a short distance from the Ecorse Municipal Boat Ramp on High Street and Biddle.

ECORSE • At the foot of Southfield and toward the south, the John D. Dingell Park provides a long line of benches for ship watchers and offshore fishermen, plus the above-mentioned facility for boaters.

RIVER ROUGE • A neat little riverside park at the end of Belanger Park Drive with boat launch site, picnic and playground aids, and a guard on duty. Free to residents; nonresidents pay $3.00.

DETROIT

FIND yourself a comfortable bench in Windsor's (Ontario, Canada) Dieppe Park and gaze straight across the river at the glassy, glossy towers of the Renaissance Center, the City National Building (which will always be the Penobscot Building to older Detroiters), and other twentieth-century monoliths. This is the best view of the Detroit skyline and a favorite spot for photographers.

The settlement that started it all, Cadillac's Fort Pontchartrain, took up less space than one floor of any of the high-risers before you. The first building within its gates was a little log church, 24½' × 35', dedicated to St. Anne. The present St. Anne's is not far from the original site.

Some of the founding colonists had property inside the stockade, while others were granted land outside the fort—long thin strips designed to give everyone access to the river. Names of early "ribbon" farm owners (the plots were 200 feet wide and 3 miles deep) are familiar today as Detroit street titles: Beaubien, Dequindre, and Campau are samples.

For fifty-nine years the French were in charge. Then the 1760 defeat of the French by the British at Montreal put Canada and such possessions as Fort Ponchartrain under a new flag...a change the Indians seem to have taken even harder than the French.

As France's fur-trading monopoly vanished, crafty independent traders roamed the woods, cheating tribesmen without conscience, selling them watered whiskey and shoddy goods. Adding insult to these injuries, the new British officers tried to impose their own military discipline on the natives, fueling the anger and conspiracy of Chief Pontiac, leader of the Ottawas. Pontiac was a powerful, compelling personality, and a genius at strategy; Fort Detroit (as it was called by then) barely survived his 153-day siege.

PLAN A CANADIAN CAPER

Windsor, Detroit's sister city to the *south* (look at the map) is loaded with good restaurants, unusual shopping, and some very interesting things to see and do...besides being a superb vantage point for photographing Detroit. It's very simple to get over and back, and whether you go via the tunnel or the bridge, you are just blocks away from the riverfront, Cleary Auditorium, the University of Windsor, and more.

TIPS: Although crossing the border is easy, always have two or three sources of personal identification ready...just in case.

—A U.S. citizen may bring back $300 worth of goods, duty-free, after a Canadian stay of forty-eight hours—and not a *minute* less. This may not be done more than once in any thirty-day period, although family members can combine their duty-free allotments.

—If you stay for less than forty-eight hours you may bring home a duty-free purchase of no more than $25.00, and in this case you *cannot* combine your allotment with other family members.

—For complete customs information call U.S. Customs 313/226-3141 or Canadian Customs 519/254-9202.

—Tunnel and Bridge both cost one dollar for car, passengers, and driver. This is also the rate for an empty pick-up truck, camper truck, and personal motor home. To pull a trailer—travel, boat, or utility—is another fifty cents. Tariffs are subject to change. (Don't feel like driving over? Go by bus! For driving or busing information call Detroit-Windsor Tunnel 313/963-8220.)

For Canadian travel assistance visit the tourist center near the Tunnel entrance in Windsor, or write Canadian Government Office of Tourism, 1900 First Federal Building, 1001 Woodward Avenue, Detroit, Michigan 48226.

The American stars and stripes went up Detroit's flagpole in 1792, although the whole place was surprisingly surrendered back to the British for a year in 1812.

Fire, the scourge of all things wooden, was the next big battle. When John Harvey went to put out his pipe in 1805, some ashes started a pile of straw burning and 299 out of 300 community structures went up in the swiftly-spreading blaze.

The damage was devastating, but it gave city fathers a chance to redesign the town layout. Having streets radiate out from central points seemed like a grand idea and thereafter Detroit's map was basically a wheel instead of a grid. Prophetic, perhaps.

Another corner was turned in 1818 when a new-fangled steam marvel dubbed the *Walk-in-the-Water* puffed its way up from Buffalo without a single sail to the wind. The new breed of ship had paddle wheels and black belching smoke—but was it *fast*! In twenty years over thirty-six steamers a day were wheezing up to Detroit's docks, loaded with visitors, easterners with one-way tickets, and immigrants from across the seas. By the time of the Civil War the city was about twentieth in size in the nation; big enough to muster 6,000 young men to the Union cause.

With thousands of incoming Germans, Poles, Italians, and others putting their imprint on the city's character, Detroit became a major manufacturing center long before automobiles turned it into the Motor City. Shoes, pharmaceuticals, salt, seeds, and stoves had Detroit labels. However, when the auto assembly lines took shape and Henry Ford announced a block-busting $5.00-a-day wage, the exploding auto job market pulled workers from other industries, from the nations' farms and towns as well as from overseas. True or not, Detroit took on the reputation of a one-product town.

One of the unhappy side effects of heavy industrialism was the image of a city with tools in its hands and not much on its mind. This narrow stereotype paid little attention to the exceptionally fine symphony orchestra, one of the nation's top art collections, an outstanding library, two major universities, and much more. Today the Detroit Concert Band is selling recordings around the world, the old but acoustically perfect Orchestra Hall is ringing with new vigor, and theater arts are thriving. There is no reason for anyone to hold to the cultural-backwash view of Detroit.

Nearly 400 lakes, streams, and parks are within an hour's drive of the city, but visitor's are urged to go first to the *Hart* of it all ... Hart Plaza down on the waterfront adjoining the Cobo convention facilities, Ford Auditorium, and the Renaissance Center. Ride the trolley, walk to Hudson's Department Store, explore "Ren Cen." Here are some Detroit details, starting with near downtown and along the river:

RENAISSANCE • CENTER

Ren Cen to its friends, an unmissable complex of tall tubular towers along the river; a mega-center of shops, offices, restaurants, and the world's tallest hotel. The outside rises like the Emerald City of Oz done up in gray glass, while some of the interior intriguingly resembles a chain of caverns with sidewalk bazaars in the hollows.

You can't wander through Ren Cen in a straight line. Walkways gently arc around a high atrium and over short bridges for views of hanging tapestries, greenery, and diners. Getting lost is easier than spending money, but an army of uniformed attendants stands ready to enlighten the confused. It's all part of the fun.

Spending money, however, *can* be done through a tight fist. Twenty eateries for fifty kinds of budgets means you can go for Greek, Japanese, French, health food, Big Boy, Big Mac, or settle for a bagel. Duchess-types will delight in the Paris designer shops, common folks have bargain racks in ready-to-wear, and everybody who has ever rubbed one nickle against another will be interested in the Money Museum, Tower 2, street level.

Ren Cen's Westin Hotel (once the Plaza), rises seventy-two stories, thus taking the hospitality business to new world heights. Trivia fans note that the hotel's 1400 guest rooms makes for a laundry list of over three million sheets, pillow cases, and towels a year. You are given these and other statistical gems when you pay the dollar for a ride to the Summit (lounge, dining) on one of the "outside" elevators. Don't skip it. There are marvelous places at the top to sit and enjoy the farthest view in Michigan. For more details, call 313/568-8282.

Detroit's Renaissance Center

Inside the Ren Cen

This historic house of worship, built specifically for crewmen on the lakes, was moved *en toto* from its original site on Woodward Avenue to its present location next to Hart Plaza. Every service begins with the Navy hymn; everyone is welcome to stop by.

● MARINER'S CHURCH

On Riopelle and Wilkins just north of Gratiot, it's easily recognized by the big bird and baloney graphics. Detroit's fresh-from-the-farm (or the sea, lake, cheese factory, sausage works, etc.) market with over 100 stalls selling the makings of a thousand feasts. A Saturday morning must.

● EASTERN MARKET

Authentic Greek restaurants and stores cram the Monroe block between Beaubien and St. Antoine, offering shish kebab, flaming cheese, and baklava straight from Mt. Olympus. Detroit Greeks have nurtured this little slice of their heritage with unusual care; it's more than a neighborhood—it's a Motown institution.

● GREEKTOWN

Bright red trolleys imported from Portugal swing and sway merrily from Ren Cen past Hart Plaza, Cobo Hall, the Convention Center, and on up to Washington Boulevard. Only twenty-five cents for the minitour.

● TROLLEY RIDES

Generations of Detroiters have regarded a summer without a trip to Bob Lo (Bois Blanc) as duller than a birthday without cake. The island fell to seedy times for a number of years, but has been spruced up, furnished with fun rides, restaurants, and excellent shows while still retaining grassy picnic areas and serene spots for asphalt escapees. Unused and ghostly, the shell of the once-grandest ballroom of its kind in North America still stands ... for those who seek clues to earlier days. Gardens, roller coasters, and a Petting Zoo for the kids speak of a brand new era.

● BOB LO, BOATS, ET AL.

Antiques of their genre, the *St. Clair* and *Columbia* are constantly inspected and declared as safe as your living room. Four times a day one of them leaves the dock near Cobo Hall (six sailings on Saturday) for more than an hour of river sight-seeing ... a marvelous show in itself. The steamers have plenty of walking-around space, chairs, refreshments, a dance floor, and a souvenir stand. Big bands play every Friday night on the moonlight cruise. (Names like Glen Miller, Woody Herman, etc. Old but magic.) Under four years, free; four to eleven, $7.00; twelve to sixty-one, $8.00. An unlimited ride ticket may be purchased on the island for $5.00, or plan ahead and get the bargain all-in-one ticket: children $9.75, adults $12.50. Subject to change.

Bob-Lo is Canadian-owned. Break their rules and you may have to go through customs plus red tape to get back. For information call 313/962-9622 or 964-5775 (U.S.); 519/255-1271 or 255-1272 (Canadian).

Close to downtown:

DETROIT CULTURAL • One of the nation's largest cultural complexes features sixteen
CENTER institutions focusing on everything from outer space to antique toys. In the "center de center" the **Detroit Institute of Arts** and the **Detroit Public Library**, two Italianate giants, stand straight across from each other about one-and-one-half miles north of the river on Woodward Avenue.

The Art Institute owns a top-rated collection of European and American masters, antiquities, Indian and African art, and more. Lunch in the Kresge Court is a treat. Sunday morning "Brunch with Bach" (music and quiche) or jazz in the afternoon is even better. Open Tues.-Sun., 9:30–5:30. Donation. Closed Mondays and holidays. 313/833-7900.

The Library is Michigan's finest, an enormous spread of volumes for research or browsing. See the giant world globe in the Cass Avenue lobby. Tours available on advanced request. 313/833-1000.

DETROIT SCIENCE • Newest addition to the museum list, this one features hands-on
CENTER and you-work-it displays plus an exciting Space Theater. 52 E. Forest (one short block from Art Institute). Sun. 12:00–5:00; Mon.-Fri. 9:00–5:00; Sat. 10:00–5:00. 313/833-1892.

DETROIT • The Detroit scene from its early French settlement days to the
HISTORICAL MUSEUM near present in sprightly displays. Everybody loves the nineteenth-century street realistically reproduced to let you walk on the cob-

blestones and peek into shop windows. Sun. 1:00–5:00; Tues., Thurs., Fri., Sat. 9:30–5:30; Wed. 1:00–9:00.

A life-sized laughing horse made entirely of chrome auto bumpers (how's that for mixed symbolism?) stands out in front of a stately old house, home of this collection that's not for children only. Natural history exhibits, ethnic heritage displays, a planetarium, and more. Mon.-Fri. 1:00–4:00, Sat. 9:00–4:00. 313/494-1210. North side of Kirby, straight across from the Art Institute.

● THE CHILDREN'S MUSEUM

Next door to the above, this is a cultural and learning center for all people, especially new Americans. The main hall is a showcase for the arts and handicrafts of the world community, the lower level has classrooms and a cozy lunchroom swimming with old world aromas. Open weekdays. Browse through the small overseas gift shop while you're there. 313/871-8600.

● INTERNATIONAL INSTITUTE

A beautiful 1888 Victorian mansion at 110 E. Ferry, filled with crafts and classes. 313/871-1667. The **Center for Creative Studies**, 245 E. Kirby, has a playfully open design and very good student-faculty shows. Or try the **Wayne State University Art School** about two blocks west.

● YOUR HERITAGE HOUSE

On the near east side:

Initially purchased from the Indians for three rolls of tobacco, eight barrels of rum, six pounds of red paint, and one belt of wampum; much later (1879) it was sold to the city for $200,000 ... over the violent protests of many citizens. It had been an offshore pigpen for early settlers who wanted to keep their pork safe from mainland wolves. The pigs thrived, went wild, and "Hog Island" was no place for a picnic. The city, however, brought in a famous designer of parks, F. L. Olmstead, who turned the property into a splendid park, one of the nation's top municipal getaways—for one hundred years the place to have family reunions, play ball, fish, ride horses, and hold hands.

Three miles from downtown, you'll find a golf course, nature

● BELLE ISLE

center, canoe rentals, shore fishing, and buggy rides. Three special attractions: the **Belle Isle Zoo,** a new design letting you walk above the critters on African-style bridges. Emphasis on baby animals. 10:00–5:30 daily, April through October. Admission. For an eyeball-to-eyeball look at some of the creatures you may hope to catch, the **Belle Isle Aquarium** charges no fee, has local and exotic specimens. 313/824-3223. The plant conservatory in an adjacent building is especially fun to wander through just before Christmas or Easter. On the south edge of the shore the **Dossin Great Lakes Museum** is filled with ship models, a small wheelhouse, the woodwork of a "gothic" salon from an old-time luxury cruiser, and other bits and pieces from the marine viewpoint. Except for a brief period in late December and early January, the museum is open all year, Wed.-Sun. 10:00–5:30. Free-will admission. 313/267-6440.

On the near west side:

THE AFRO-● | The museum houses African artifacts, files on famous black people,
AMERICAN MUSEUM | and a black art collection. 1553 W. Grand Boulevard (corner of
OF DETROIT | Warren). Tues.-Fri. 9:00–5:00; Sat. 10:00–4:00. 313/899-2500.

FORT WAYNE● The best-preserved pre–Civil War fortification in America guards its treasures on Jefferson Avenue near Livernois, west from downtown. Almost hidden by the surrounding industry, Fort Wayne's green glacis (earthen embankments) would make you think it's not there ... except for the signs. Once past these barriers you find the brick-walled fort that never knew a war, never fired a shot. Casements, battle stations, gun placements, and barracks double as a museum of fort and city history. Don't miss the Indian Museum just beyond the west gate, all included in the modest admission price.

Of special Detroit-area interest:

THE DETROIT ZOO● A miniature train toots through a tunnel and emerges in South Africa for eye contact with lions, tigers, bears, and whatsthats. The great apes have a building of their own; so do reptiles, birds, and penquins . . . although all are indoors for winter visitors. Large area for picnics, several refreshment spots. Open Wed.-Sun. 10:00–4:00. 313/398-0900 (will give Belle Isle information also).

The largest collection of Americana anywhere. The fourteen-acre ● GREENFIELD
Museum reflects farm, home, industrial, and transport develop- VILLAGE AND THE
ment, while the Village is an assemblage of famous homes, historic HENRY FORD
work sites, a steam train, and amusement park. Edison's laboratory, MUSEUM
Noah Webster's house, the Wright brothers' home; it makes for
quite a neighborhood. Muzzle loaders, antique car collectors, and
fife and drum groups fill the calendar with summer rallies and
special events. Take I-94 to Southfield exit or Michigan Avenue to
Oakland. Open every day but Thanksgiving, Christmas, and New
Year's Day. Museum admission: $7.00 for adults, $3.50 children
six to twelve; Village, $8.00 adults, $4.00 children six to twelve,
under six free. Not exactly a budget jaunt but worth saving up for
(ask about joining the Friends for special rates). Summer hours
9:00–6:00; winter 9:00–5:00. 313/271-1620.

CRANBROOK • A bright jewel among science museums is the **Institute of Science**, 500 Lone Pine Road out in Bloomfield Hills. Planetarium, gem-mineral display, natural dioramas, hands-on physics exhibits, and more. Closed holidays, open Mon.-Fri. 10:00–5:00, Sat. 1:00–9:00, and Sun. 1:00–5:00. Admission charge. 313/645-3210.

Cranbrook Academy of Art Museum, on the same grounds, has its own collection and is the showcase for the Academy faculty and students. Special exhibitions, films, tours. Call 313/645-3312.

This abbreviated list does not include baseball at Tiger stadium (962-4000), Detroit Symphony Orchestra concerts (961-7017), sports events at the Joe Louis Arena, the summer treats at Pine Knob or Meadowbrook, or the stirring sounds of John Philip Sousa as played by the Detroit Concert Band (886-0394).

Festival toppers:
Ethnic Festivals at Hart Plaza host a different nationality group every weekend from May until mid-September; fireworks over the river highlights the Fourth of July/Dominion Day celebration, part of the International Freedom Festival; Michigan State Fair Days are at the end of August. For more information call or write the Detroit Visitor Information Center, 2 E. Jefferson Avenue, Detroit, Michigan 48226. 313/963-0879. Or try the Southeastern Michigan Travel and Tourist Association, Suite 350, American Center, 27777 Franklin Road, Southfield, Michigan. 313/357-1663.

The Detroit Memorial Park Marina across from Belle Isle has transient accommodations, restrooms, showers, holding tank pump-out, and so forth. 313/331-6511.

Boaters are advised to travel on the north side of Belle Isle (bridge clearance is thirty feet) because all commercial traffic *must* use the other channel.

SOME THINGS FISHY

A fish sees well but distance is limited due to the density of even the clearest water. When a fish looks upward, however, the surface is opaque except for a round "window" surrounding his head. (Peek into an aquarium tank from the side, look up, and see for yourself.) This hole-in-the-mirror effect is caused by the refraction of light. The fish swims to the surface to look at an object, the object magnifies as the fish gets closer, while the transparent window gets smaller. Waves and ripples break up the image, making the object appear to be wiggling disjointedly.

Judgment of distance is excellent (even though the fish is looking in two directions at once), allowing many fish to catch moving insects on flowing water while swimming rapidly themselves.

Are they color blind? Laboratory evidence shows that fish can distinguish colors, although most can't seem to tell red from purple, blue from green or black, or bright from dull.

Do they hear? Water and bone both conduct sound and it is supposed that a fish "hears" partly through its bones, air bladder, and lateral line. A few species "speak" with grunting sounds or vibrating gill covers. Sounds made by fish had to be screened out by submarine-detecting equipment used in World War II.

All species have a sense of smell, although in some fish it is much more highly developed than in others. Sharks are a nasty example of keen sniffers.

Everyone with half a heart wonders if the fish feels pain with that hook in its mouth. It is doubtful if it would pull and thrash so hard if the pain were too distracting. The fish feels discomfort, but the amount of "pain" is almost nil, may vary from one specie to another.

Fish scales are like rings on a tree. Each growth period adds to the scale, helps experts to tell a fish's age.

Why do they jump? To capture food, clear a barrier, escape an enemy, discourage a parasite. Maybe just to play.

The following brief profiles of the major catches are meant to give you an idea of when to fish, where to go, what bait to use, and what to look for—or at. If you still don't know what you caught, ask the guy who sold you the bait. (Courtesy of the Michigan Travel Bureau and the many anglers who let me peer into their creels.)

COHO Tail spots around the top of the tail, interior of mouth usually gray or black, gums are whitish. When hooked they want to roll sideways, getting entangled in line. During the spring and summer months cohos generally stay in the open water within ten miles of shore and in the upper twenty to forty feet. In late August they gather near the mouths of their parent streams and in September the upstream rush is on, snapping at lures like commuters without breakfast snap at doughnuts. If you anchor-fish, one bit of advice is to get over a hole, use action lure and dropper line.

CHINOOK (KING) Teeth set in black gums distinguish this salmon champ. The base of the tail narrows and flares, giving the angler a chance to grip the fish. Interior of mouth black or gray. Chinooks don't jump and roll as much as coho, are caught by trolling and mooching on open water, casting or anchor fishing in streams. In open water they stay closer to the bottom than their coho cousins. Ten- to thirty-pound chinook are mighty nice to bring in; specimens of over fifty pounds have been caught.

STEELHEAD Interior of the mouth is white, entire tail is spotted, cheek plates are a rosy shade of pink. These big silvery beauties are a kind of rainbow trout that mature in the big, deeper lakes and run again to the streams in September. Best time for stream fishing is March-April, October and November. In the deep water they like it about a mile from shore, less than fifty feet deep.

LAKE TROUT Mostly gray above and white below with diffuse creamy white spottings; tail is definitely forked. They weigh up to thirty pounds, are residents of Lake Superior and the big inland lakes such as Torch, Crystal, or Higgins. In summer they are taken by still fishing in 50 to 200 feet of water; ask about the best bait and you'll seldom get the same answer twice. Either live or dead smelt, shiner minnows, etc. Dead bait should rest on the bottom, live bait held a foot or two higher. Trollers have their own techniques. Delicious!

WALLEYE A tasty dinner fish averaging two to five pounds that runs in schools. If you catch one there's likely to be more down there. Fish the big lakes and largest inland lakes close to land points or river mouths in deep water during the summer, shallow water in spring and fall. Best warm weather results come at night.

NORTHERN PIKE Long and looking like a muskie (muskies have meaner-looking teeth, however), northerns prefer shallow reed areas in lakes where they can best prey on their own favorite suppers: fish. Northern pike strike all kinds of artificial lures, cast or trolled; are most easily taken on overcast days in early morning or after 5:00 PM. To remove slime, dip in scalding water or soak in salt water for fifteen minutes.

MUSKELLUNGE A biggie; the state hook and line record was a 62 lb., 8 oz. catch in Lake St. Clair in 1940. Michigan has two kinds of muskies. One is sometimes called the Wisconsin Musky; the other, the Great Lakes Musky, is most abundant in Lake St. Clair, the Inland Waterway, Elk Lake, and Munuscong Bay, but shows up unexpectedly almost anywhere along the Great Lakes shoreline. Both casting and trolling are done somewhat rapidly over weedbeds in spring, moving along the dropoff and into deeper water in summer. Large and active, they'll make spectacular leaps (a pose they seldom hold while you get your camera) when they've been hooked.

LARGEMOUTH BASS Look to the lily pads, among the bullrushes, around stumps and submerged logs to catch this fighting, hungry target. You are best advised to row slowly and quietly along lake edges, casting ahead of the boat into the weeds . . . at night. Have a landing net ready but don't try to bring him in too quickly. You have to play him to catch him, the experts say.

SMALLMOUTH BASS Not the kind of creature that submits when caught, the small mouth is noted for giving anglers a hard time. Look in stone or gravel areas where the water is coldest, early spring and in September or October, near the mouths of rivers and bays. In summer the smallmouth can be caught by still-fishing along the dropoff in a lake or by trolling where the bottom is rocky and the water at least ten feet deep. It takes a real fisherman to tell the smallmouth from his bigger-jawed relative.

ROCK BASS A convenient, cooperative fish that bites any time of day, (morning and evening preferred), isn't too fussy about bait but takes kindly to crayfish, minnows, grubs, and worms. Rest your hook on the bottom near underwater rockpiles, old pilings, or backwater areas of lakes and rivers.

BLACK CRAPPIE A gregarious fish that sticks to schools and wanders widely over deeper streams and lakes. Cloudy water doesn't bother them at all. Fish from ten to twenty feet deep, use a landing net because crappies have thin, easily torn mouths and can get away.

BLUEGILL Found nearly everywhere in the state. There's no season on bluegills but the recommended time for the best catch runs from mid-May in the southern lower peninsula to late June and early July in the Upper Peninsula. During spawning they can be found in one to four feet of water along weedy stretches. Get up early for them or stay up late in the evening. Small hooks should be used, and bits of shrimp, nightcrawlers, or crickets make good bait.

PUMPKINSEED Often called Sunfish, the pumpkinseed prefers slow-moving streams, overhanging banks, and in general the same environ-ment as the bluegill. Its colors vary, but usually the pumpkinseed is a combination of greens, purple tinges, bands and stripes, and some orange spots, plus a golden belly that inspires the 'sunfish' title. Large pumps (six to eight inches) in deep cold water at midday, near dropoff or in deep lake pockets.

YELLOW PERCH One of the most popular pan fishes, sometimes known as the Ringed Perch. There's no size or season limit on these school-running creatures, best fished from twenty to fifty feet deep with a hook held a foot or so off the bottom. The spawning migration of perch in the Great Lakes means sure-catch fishing for those who drop min-nows, worms, grasshoppers, and wigglers on their lines.

RAINBOW TROUT The fish that has inspired much devoted prose, the fighting, beauteous rainbow was brought to Michigan from far western streams. Most of them are, in reality, migratory steelhead spending their first years in streams, maturing in the big lakes and returning to

spawn. Use worms, flashing spinners, and dark streamers at depths of fifteen to twenty-five feet.

BROOK TROUT Tasty, dainty, and wary. Approach quietly the deep holes, beaver dams, and submerged logs where they linger. Lots of patience and hope recommended; fly fishermen and worm fishermen have different ideas about what works best.

BROWN TROUT Browns can be found in a majority of Michigan streams and in deep cold lakes. They are cautious fellows most easily taken very early in the morning, after sundown or dark, and after a heavy rainstorm where the waters of normally clear streams have been muddied. You are told to allow plenty of slack line, that when a brown feels the line drag he will spit out the bait.

CARP Goldfish without the gold, carp lead quiet lives near piles of driftwood, shallow lakes, and streams. A catch weighing twenty pounds is not uncommon. Use angleworms, peeled crayfish tails, corn, or even boiled potatoes. May be taken with dip nets during May and from some waters with spear or bow and arrow. Be sure you check with your fishing guide first.

SUCKERS There's one hatched every minute . . . undoubtedly more. In spring when their meat is firm they are a good sport and food source. Most folks go after suckers with a bamboo pole, line, sinker, and angleworm, fishing from a shore-based camp chair.

BULLHEADS With faces only other bullheads could love, the fishes with the strange beards stick to quiet waters, sluggish streams, and shallow lakes. A big one might weigh five pounds but the smaller ones are said to be tastier. Go after bullheads in the summer night or in daytime after a rain . . . and be careful; those sharp spines on the dorsal and pectoral fins can cause painful cuts. Clean, skin with a pair of pliers, then fry in deep fat.

SMELT Why won't you see this silvery little rascal listed in the fishing guides? Because only in the spring when it comes in from the big lakes to spawn close to shore is the smelt within the grasp of fishermen. Strictly a dip-netting operation early in April, smelt is too widely dispersed to pay attention to after that.

WHITEFISH Menus read "Lake Superior Whitefish"—so why isn't this succulent delicacy listed on the fishing guides? It is for the commercial experts to catch, that's why. Its thin mouth membranes do not hold the bait; as a sportsman's fish the dinnertime special doesn't handle well.

ST. CLAIR STATISTICS

Length	26 miles
Width	24 miles
Length of coastline including Canada and islands	257 miles
Total water surface	490 square miles
United States water surface	198 square miles
Total land drainage basin	6,930 square miles
United States drainage	2,850 square miles
Maximum depth	21 feet
Average depth	10 feet
Volume of water	1 cubic mile

LAKE ST. CLAIR
and the
ST. CLAIR RIVER

I F you squint at the map and use a little imagination you can see
why Lake St. Clair is called the "heart" of the lakes. It has that
romantic shape: pointed at the bottom and curving in toward itself
at the top. Never more than twenty-six feet deep (where it's been
dredged), St. Clair is twenty-six miles from north to south, twenty-
four miles from east to west.

There are conflicting tales concerning its saintly name. Some
say that LaSalle came up to the lake on the ill-fated *Griffin* (it
later sank in Lake Michigan without a trace) and named the water
body after his heavenly patron. The truth has more to do with
General Arthur St. Clair, last president of the Continental Congress
and first governor of the Northwest Territory . . . the real honoree.

Canada has a bit more than our sixty-two miles of shoreline,
but it would be hard to beat the mix 'n' match of the Michigan
side: Elegant homes and swank yacht basins near Detroit and
Windmill Point; innumerable canals and marinas of St. Clair Shores;
the huge Metropolitan Beach complex complete with swamps and
marshes; an active Air Force base; thousands of cottages, small
communities, wildlife refuges, and so forth.

Although not considered to be one of the *great* lakes, St. Clair
more than earns her popularity for top fishing and boating.

In local jargon "fishing the flats" means trying to outwit the
walleye, perch, bass, and a sizeable list of others in the delta area
where the St. Clair River enters the lake. The river branches into
three main channels—easily remembered as the North, Middle,

31

and South—forming large and small islands. Since the South Channel is used by large commercial vessels, smaller craft are advised to use the other routes when possible.

Harsen's Island is the largest on the Michigan side of the border, a name that has conjured up visions of easy summer living for generations of Detroiters who own cottages there. Across from Harsen's the Walpole Island Indian Reservation lands form the largest section of the flats.

For twenty-seven miles, from Algonac to Port Huron, the St. Clair River offers marvelous vantage points for ship-watchers with roads close to the shore on both sides of the border. Car ferries at Algonac, Marine City, and St. Clair will take you across; bobbing little tug-like boats that are fun rides in and of themselves.

As you watch the river from a park bench or over the ferry rail you'll probably comment on the swiftness of the current. Velocity is about 5 mph at Port Huron and drops to $1\frac{1}{2}$ mph in the lower channel. However, if that swift look discourages you from trying to swim in it, all the better; the St. Clair River must cope with ship wakes and industrial problems. It is not for swimmers.

WINDMILL POINT • The 90-mile circuit along the water from Detroit to Port Huron begins at this gentle peninsula. In 1723, just eleven years after Fort Pontchartrain was founded, this was the scene of the bloodiest fracas in Michigan history. Wisconsin Foix and Sauk Indians (encouraged by the English) laid siege to the Fort, fighting against Hurons and Ottawas—friends of the French. After three weeks 1200 Sauk and Foix surrendered and then were slaughtered; one of the worst massacres on the frontier.

Today the steel tower at the Point is visible for fourteen miles out on Lake St. Clair and the dedicatedly serene Grosse Pointe communities combine in a gold-plated lake front. Jefferson Avenue becomes Lake Shore Drive for a while and is an exceedingly pleasant, no-parking road.

ST. CLAIR SHORES • A water-loving town where marinas are clustered near the lake like fast food chains near a mall, and dozens of canals bring access rights to the back door of a thousand homes. If you stay on Jef-

ferson you'll see places to ask for boat rentals and fishing information.

Run by the Huron-Clinton Metropolitan Authority, the park offers • METROPOLITAN/
more than twenty recreational options from tot-lots to a dance   BEACH PARK
pavillion with live bands on summer weekends. Naturally this
makes it quite a drawing card on hot July days; Metro gets crowded,
but there's a lot of room and on chilly or rainy days it's a real
retreat.

For boaters there are facilities for launching all trailerable craft,
plus transient accommodations for boats coming in from the lake.
Showers, tank pump-outs, and so forth.

Metro's paved hike/bike trails curve past the wetlands area, a
Mississippi-style riverboat stop, miniature golf, and the central fo-
cus: an enormous beach with bathhouse and refreshment stand.
A 3/4-mile trail lets you get close to the cattails, herons, redwinged blackbirds and other flora/fauna of the marshy kind.

To get there take the Metro Parkway east off I-94; $2.00 daily
entrance fee or $7.00 per season.

Running through the heart of Mt. Clemens, the county seat of • THE CLINTON RIVER
Macomb County, the Clinton River empties into Lake St. Clair just
north of Metro Park. A favorite with canoeists who can paddle
upstream for many miles but are warned not to enter the big lake.
Call 853-6156 for canoe rental information or write Metro Beach
Park, P.O. Box 1037, Mt. Clemens, Michigan 48043.

At the east end of M-59, with a cement ramp, parking for 155 cars, • SELFRIDGE FIELD
and special site rules. Mt. Clemens, exit east off I-94.   ACCESS SITE

This isn't exactly a coastline city but it's close enough. Once • MOUNT CLEMENS
known for its cure-all mineral baths and health spas, the town
boasts a lovely library, a symphony orchestra, an art center, and
wondrous items like the biggest bust of John F. Kennedy anywhere. The Macomb County Historical Museum, 15 Union Street,
is an old Victorian house listed in the state's registry of historic
sites.

Big events include ethnic festivals on weekends, the September Farm Market, and the terrifically exciting annual air show at the Selfridge Air National Guard Base (date varies).

The Air National Guard Base at Selfridge Field has a fledgling Military Air Museum going. Models, pictures, gear, and more trace the history of the seventy-five-year-old airfield where Coast Guard, Marines, Air Force Reserve, and Naval units have been stationed. Outside the small museum building a row of grounded oldies seem ready to fight again. Open every Tues. and Thurs., also 1st and 3rd Sundays of each month, 1:00–5:00 PM. Donation. 313/466-5035. Base tours are available for groups of ten or more with advance reservations. Write to Public Relations, Selfridge A.N.G. Base, Mt. Clemens, Michigan 48043, or Mt. Clemens County Chamber of Commerce, 31½ N. Walnut Street, Mt. Clemens 48043.

BRANDENBURG •
MEMORIAL PARK AND
ACCESS SITE

A nice place for a picnic or to launch your boat. Operated by New Baltimore Township on the south side of New Baltimore off Jefferson Avenue. Swings, swimming, and all facilities for any trailerable boat. You'll be easing into the Anchor Bay section of Lake St. Clair.

FAIR HAVEN •

Another hard-surface ramp into Anchor Bay, this one has parking for 100 cars, toilets, and so forth.

ST. JOHN'S MARSH •
WILDLIFE AREA

Migratory birds and birds that spend the winter, plus abundant opportunities for shorefishing right next to the inland side of M-29 (Dyke Road) draw folks to this watery stretch. A zillion nearby cottages and everybody fishes, so boat rentals and bait stores are not hard to find.

HARSEN'S ISLAND •

The St. Clair Flats Wildlife Area takes up nearly half of this popular resort island. Main community is Sans Souci. Although their numbers diminish in winter, the residents who live here year-round like their icy isolation. That accounts for the lack of a bridge. You must ferry across, $1.50 round trip.

The island access site has a hard-surface ramp but the water depth is limited and retrieving a large craft could be a problem.

The ferry to Harsen's Island leaves from here, a good little town • ALGONAC
for a dinner and ship-watching stop. There's a city-run access site
with parking for forty cars, facilities, and an all-trailerable-boats
ramp.

The number of places to watch the long ships increases as you
drive north along the St. Clair River.

On M-29, 300 campsites on over a thousand acres. *No* swimming, • ALGONAC STATE
boating, launch sites, or park store, but a *great* place to review   PARK
the parade of big boats. All comfort facilities, hiking trails, fishing,
and hunting.

A tidy little river town that seems to stay the same year after • MARINE CITY
year—nice. A ferry will take you across to Sombra, Ontario, if
you'd like to drive on the Canadian side for a while. The Marine
City–Belle River access site has a ramp suitable for canoes and
small boats, no larger craft (for upstream paddling only; the St.
Clair River is no place for canoes).

Another neat community with lovely old houses and a waterfront • ST. CLAIR
park with benches facing those facinating freighters, St. Clair boasts
of some interesting shops and a classic among riverside hotels,
the memorable St. Clair Inn. In the Historical Museum, a former
Baptist Church at 308 S. Fourth Street, they've got the desk of the
man responsible for our custom of flying the U.S. flag over school-
houses(!) plus antique toys, and more. Open Fri.-Sun. 1:30–4:30
and by appointment.

At this point the ferry crosses to Courtright, Ontario. A boat
harbor *and* access site can be found at the St. Clair Dock, Pine
and St. Clair rivers (just west of Riverside and south—across
bridge—of Clinton Avenue). Transient accommodations for incoming boats, showers, gasoline, holding tank pump-out, and so
forth. 313/329-4125.

On up the River Road (M-29 ends, M-25 takes over), on through
Marysville (note parks and river-viewing spots), and you are in
Port Huron, gateway town to the big-sea water.

GETTING TO KNOW THE LONG SHIPS

At 700 to 1000 feet long, many of the freighters plying the Great Lakes are longer than the Washington Monument is tall. They glide past the viewer with liquid grace; iron fortresses on a glistening track. Only when one of them lets out a sudden deep and startling signal to another ship can you hear it at all.

During the peak of the summer shipping season an average of sixty freighters per day can be seen on the Detroit River or going through the Soo locks. Most are "lakers" bearing company names such as *U.S. Steel* or *Medusa Cement*. The rest are "salties," their identities often obscured in unfamiliar alphabets.

Lakers Until recently lake freighters were built with the wheelhouse (pilothouse or bridge) at the bow (front) and the engine room, crew's quarters, and so forth at the stern (back). These vessels are generally longer and lower than salties, have flatter sides and use loading gear that folds and rests less conspicuously on the deck.

The newest lakers, however, are built with an eye to better function. Wheelhouse, quarters, and the rest have been combined in one large five- or six-story structure at the stern; sides, bow, and stern have been made even flatter and everything possible has been done to enlarge cargo capacity while consolidating work areas.

Storm waves on the Great Lakes are choppy, irregular, erratic. Lake ships, confined to narrow shipping channels, have little room to maneuver about and therefore are built with a certain flexibility to cope with the sidewise pounding they often take. For this reason lakers do not venture out into the high seas where rolling swells put a different kind of stress on hulls.

Salties To the unschooled landlubber (including this writer) ships with their superstructure centered firmly astern have an awkward look. We like to think the best place for the captain—like a motorist—is up front. Salties are stacked in the stern and are usually festooned with unloading equipment, folded like so many enormous grasshopper legs along the deck.

Almost all overseas vessels will fly the American and Canadian flag as a courtesy to the countries they are passing between. The flag of the country the ship is registered under and pays dues to will be flapping off the stern.

At night there's another way to tell lakers from salters; the foreign ships are almost dark compared to the extravagantly lit local vessels.

Companies and Countries The name of the ship is always painted on both sides of the bow and across the stern. Also on the stern is the name of the port city of the ship's home country such as Kobe (Japan), Patras (Greece), Montreal, or New York. Real ship-watching experts can tell ownership by the stack markings, the stripes and letters on the funnel. A red funnel with two white and one blue line belongs to the Imperial Oil Ltd. of Toronto; black with a white band and red star means a Yugoslavian ship is passing. A booklet called *Know Your Ships* is available at the Dossin Museum on Belle Isle, the S.S. *Valley Camp* at the Soo, and several other places, listing in full color all the flags and stacks of vessels now going through the Seaway plus a great deal of further information. To order: Marine Publishing Company, Inc., P.O. Box 68, Sault Ste. Marie, Michigan 49783. $3.50 for American handling and postage, $4.00 Canadian.

What Are They Saying?

1 long = I am directing my course to starboard (right)
2 long = I am heading to port (left)
2 short, one or 2 long = greetings between sister ships plus direction
5 or more short rapid blasts = *danger*. During a heavy fog the Coast Guard requires a ship to sound one long blast every 60 seconds. In fog too thick for navigation, the ship anchors and rings a bell every sixty seconds.

If you go fishing, doze off, and hear 5 blasts close by, wake up in a hurry; you're in real trouble.

1 long blast lasting 8 or more seconds = leaving the dock
2 long, 2 short = call for dispatch to American locks
3 long, 2 short = call for dispatch to Canadian locks
2 short = stop ship in lock or at dock with winches and propeller
1 short = cast off lines at dock or in lock
3 long, 2 short = salute
3 short = ship moving in fog; check speed
1 long, 2 short = master salute
1 long, 2 long and 1 short = I am at anchor

Lights on the Subject Two running lights are colored, a red light on the port side, a green light on the starboard (right), and the rest are always white. The masthead light is at the bow of the ship, on or in front of the foremast. It shines dead ahead and very slightly to each side. Another light at the stern, called the range light, is higher than the bow light and shines in *all* directions. If you can see *both* colored lights *and* two high white lights, the ship is coming straight toward you. Row faster!

If a ship is towing another boat, it will have two white lights on the bow mast about six feet apart. If the cargo is flammable, a red light will be hung below the top light.

A large ship going through the water is a thing of beauty . . . and nothing to tease. They *cannot* stop quickly or dodge small boats. Getting too close in small craft is an exceedingly DUMB chance to take.

Finally, I share my secret for keeping "port" and "starboard" straight. *Port* and *left* both have four letters and therefore are a match.

38

SAULT STE. MARIE
Sugar Island
ST. IGNACE
Neebish Island
CEDARVILLE
HESSEL
Drummond Island
DETOUR VILLAGE
Mackinac Island
Bois Blanc Island
CHEBOYGAN
MACKINAW CITY
ROGERS CITY
ALPENA
HARRISVILLE
OSCODA
AU SABLE
TAWAS CITY
PORT AUSTIN
GRINDSTONE CITY
PORT HOPE
OMER
STANDISH
CASEVILLE
PINCONNING
BAY PORT
HARBOR BEACH
LINWOOD
SEBEWAING
BAY CITY
PORT SANILAC
LEXINGTON
PORT HURON

PART TWO

LAKE HURON

PORT HURON TO BAY CITY; NORTH TO CHEBOYGAN;
MACKINAW CITY TO DRUMMOND ISLAND;
DETOUR VILLAGE TO SAULT STE. MARIE

LAKE HURON STATISTICS

Length in miles from mouth of St. Mary's River to head of St. Clair River	223 miles
Breadth	183 miles
Length of coastline including Canada and islands	3,830 miles
Total water surface	23,050 square miles
United States water surface	9,150 square miles
Total land drainage basin	51,700 square miles
United States drainage	16,200 square miles
Maximum depth	750 feet
Average depth	195 feet
Volume of water	849 cubic miles

LAKE HURON

PORT Huron's Fort Gratiot lighthouse, aging sentry to Lake Huron's southern gate, is the first object in Michigan to be touched by the light of the rising sun. It beams toward the second largest of the lakes, bigger than the states of Vermont, New Hampshire, and Connecticut combined.

When the earliest white explorers, Jesuit missionaries and voyageurs, came out of Georgian Bay into Lake Huron, they fully expected the waters to turn salty as they pressed ahead, convinced that these blue horizons were shared with China. The newcomers named their shining discovery "La Mer Douce," the Sweet Sea, which later became Huron, a name the French bestowed upon the local Indians.

The ice age's advancing and retreating glaciers nearly made Lakes Michigan and Huron into mirror images, but the formation of what is now Saginaw Bay altered Huron's southern contours. There are other differences, too. Lake Michigan has a long chain of lakes just inland from its coast (Macatawa, Pentwater, Muskegon, Crystal, Torch, to name a few) that have made ideal natural harbors and encouraged both commercial and recreational development. Huron has no similar chain, nor has it the high dunes of the western coast, although the eastern shore has superlative beaches.

Port Huron, Sarnia (Ontario, Canada), and Bay City are the largest communities with Lake Huron frontage, although Saginaw—just upstream—is close to the scene. But this is not quite a counterpart to Milwaukee, Gary, Chicago, Muskegon, and the

41

others, which should mean that Huron is not subject to the heavy use and abuse Lake Michigan gets. The problems are not to be underestimated, however.

Experienced boatmen tell tales of each lake's separate navigational personality, whimsical currents, and sudden storms that quickly teach saltwater sailors not to scoff at the problems of "inland" skippers. Riding the cold autumnal lakes, fresh water rains quickly freeze into a burden of ice, and the narrow shipping lanes allow little room for maneuvering against short (comparatively) choppy waves. Scores of vessels have been lost in Lake Huron; eight vanished in one storm without a single survivor. These past calamities now draw hundreds of scuba divers to the waters at the south end of the lake and to the Alpena region especially ... to a point where an underwater "park" to preserve what is left has been considered.

THE GLORIOUS GREAT LAKES
Quote from Noel Mostert, *Holiday* Magazine

... the most splendid phenomenon on the face of the earth. ...."

"Most people when they first see the Great Lakes are startled because they have forgotten that the lakes exist, and they think the sky has fallen. My own first introduction to them some years ago was along the spectacular stretch of Canadian Pacific track that runs along the north shore of Superior.

The train comes drumming down from the bushland plateau, the crimson cars double and turn in the cuttings, flashing against the cedars, past black bear on one rock and gulls on another, slowly making the hairpin jackknife curve, and the water, as emerald as any Pacific atoll's, heaves below with the weight of great distance behind it, and you look up from the waves spreading on the white empty sands to the horizon vast and open as the sea. I retain my wonder of that horizon because the Great Lakes have always struck me as being by far the truest measure of North America's breadth, hard to grasp that a land should contain several fresh-water seas so big that ships can steam out of sight on the shore for a day or more, or even founder in giant waves. ...

Used by permission of TRAVEL/HOLIDAY,
Travel Bldg, Floral Park, New York.

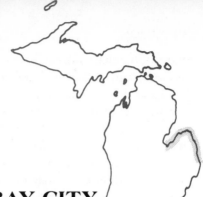

PORT HURON TO BAY CITY

FOR map-clear reasons this region of Michigan is called the Thumb. It could also be called the "bean jar," the "milk pail," or the "sugar bowl." Nearly all of the world's white navy beans come from Thumb counties, Michigan's milk production centers in Sanilac County, and the granulated beet business is so sweet they have a sugar festival every year.

Our subpeninsula is good at folksy festivals, fairs, and family reunions. The annual Farmer's Festival in Pigeon (usually the last weekend in July), for example, is mid-America at its traditional and down-home best; high school bands march, the Jaycees parade in floats dreamed up over breakfast coffee, there's a quilt show at the library, a pancake and sausage supper in the park, a baby crawl contest, sidewalk sales, frog-jumping bees, and general fun.

In Parisville, the oldest Polish Catholic parish in the state holds a reunion every summer that's like a gathering of the clan. Everybody goes. For its share, Bay Port declares a "Fish Sandwich Day"; in Caseville thousands flock to an annual art show. Those who circle the Thumb are amiss if they don't grab a copy of the nearest town paper to find out what's going on.

Yet the pervading atmosphere of the area is serenity, of having nothing to do but relax. The heavy industry south of Port Huron is gone, along with the traffic and crowds. M-25 follows the water's edge fairly closely and there are plenty of places to park for a long look at the water . . . outward and down. Much of the Lake Huron side of the Thumb is a rather high bluff.

A trio of disasters have affected the coast you see today. Two were horrendous fires that swept across much of Michigan in 1871 and 1881, doing lethal damage to the lower half of the state and particularly to the Thumb. In 1871, close to the day that the Chicago fire and Wisconsin's Prestigo fires broke out, the tinder-dry lumber camps of Bad Axe and Pigeon burned, towns and settlements were wiped out, hundred of lives were lost, and the economy ground to a halt. There were still trees, however (Michigan was once a nearly unbroken forest), and lumbering continued until a second fire, ten years later, forced the switch to farming.

The other calamity was a storm on Lake Huron in 1913, a murderous November squall of such ferocity that eight freighters and several smaller boats went down with all hands on board. The same storm was dumping record snows on Cleveland and struck fiercely across Lake Superior, but shipping on Lake Huron got the worst of it. Altogether thirty-eight vessels were lost or damaged, battered by cyclone winds and an unwelcome cargo of ice.

Docking facilities of Lexington and Port Sanilac never recovered; their days as shipping ports were over. Many coastal communities have, however, new breakwaters for small craft—part of the Harbors of Refuge program.

Of interest to anthropologists and ancient history fans are the state's only petroglyphs (human carvings on rock), found on the banks of the Cass River near Holbrook in Sanilac County. Outlines of hands, mythical animals, figures of people, birds, and so forth, are all there, but unfortunately so shallow and worn that they can be seen only at dawn or dusk when the sun is casting long shadows. If you'd like to know more, write to the Cranbrook Institute of Science, Lone Pine Road, Bloomfield Hills, Michigan 48013.

Old carvings, however, do not lure the average visitor quite as much as live fish, and fishing in area streams and off-shore waters is exceptionally good. Coho and chinook salmon, steelhead and brown trout are among the prize catches. Saginaw Bay plays host to swarming conventions of perch, largemouth bass, sunfish, and northern pike. Detailed fishing information is readily available from Lansing or Bay City. Ask for the Sportsman's Guide, Log Office, Bay City, Michigan 48706; 517/895-8823. Or ask for "Fishing

in Michigan," Michigan Travel Bureau, P.O. Box 30226, Lansing, Michigan 48909. Toll free in-state, 1-800/292-2520.

As you cast your bait or sink your toes into the saltless surf, don't pass by the historic markers or zealously-kept historic collections. The gear you carry now will be in a glass case of the future.

From Lansing to the tip of the Thumb it's 149 miles; from downtown Detroit it's 124 miles. From either direction M-25 is the scenic road around the long blue edge.

The first construction here was Fort Joseph, followed by Fort Gratiot, and finally the settlement of Port Huron, one of the oldest towns in the state. The Fort Gratiot lighthouse, built in 1825, now stands where the second fort was built and is Michigan's oldest navigation light.

• PORT HURON

Racing past Fort Gratiot Lighthouse

Until the disastrous fires of 1871 changed the local economy from lumber to agriculture, Port Huron was a logging boom town. It is the first U.S. city to connect with Canada via an under-river railway tunnel, and the home of an inventive young man who worked on the Port Huron–Detroit run until he was fired for accidently setting a fire in the baggage car. That was Tom Edison.

Today Port Huron thrives on salt, boat building, paper manufacturing, and a host of other industries. A healthy pedestrian will enjoy this city with the long waterfront and the Black River parks and marinas. The *Huron Lightship*, a vessel that once guided ships into the entrance of the St. Clair River, sits on permanent exhibit at Grove Park. Open for tours on summer afternoons.

The Museum of Arts and History has a varied collection of Indian artifacts, marine paraphernalia, period furniture, natural history, and changing fine arts exhibits. 1115 Sixth Street, Wednesday through Sunday afternoons. A small donation, please.

It costs thirty-five cents per car (including passengers) to cross the high and handsome Blue Water Bridge to Sarnia; just a little more if you're pulling a trailer.

For boaters, the Port Huron mooring facility on the Black River has transient accommodations and everything else from fuel to cable TV. 313/985-5676. This is the same stream that sees the boats assembling for the Port Huron–Mackinac Island Yacht Race, a Kentucky Derby of fresh-water yachting. Watching the preparations and the parade out to the starting line near the Fort Gratiot light is a fun spectacle that draws thousands. The invitational classic highlights Port Huron's Blue Water Festival. For exact dates and further details write Greater Port Huron–Marysville Chamber of Commerce, 920 Pine Grove Avenue, Port Huron, Michigan 48060.

LAKEPORT STATE ● A tree-filled spread of 565 acres with 256 sites for campers, hot
PARK showers, and a park store to pick up the milk you forgot. The beach is grand, and a boat launch makes it easier to get at the perch. Hiking trails weave through the property. Inquire here about canoeing on the Black River.

A Harbor of Refuge stretches new arms of concrete out into the **LEXINGTON**
lake, good for walking on or fishing from—except in poor weather.
A beach, launch site, small park, marina, and ship-shaped restaurant are all at the foot of M-90. It's close to Croswell, from which
point canoeists can paddle all the way to Port Huron.

1.5 miles south of Port Sanilac, with seventeen picnic tables. **ROADSIDE PARK**

When heading north on M-25, stop at the Joseph Loop House on **PORT SANILAC**
the south side of town. A lovely Second Empire–style house that
belonged to the area's first doctor, the home is now a museum
showing off Victorian furnishings, the doctor's office, and unusual
antiques. But that's not the whole story; it includes Great Lakes
marine items, souvenirs from four wars, and natural history specimens. A dairy exhibit and restored pioneer log cabin are out
back. Open 1:00–5:00, Thursday through Sunday during the summer and fall.

More than forty buildings in Port Sanilac are over 100 years
old, a real deal for history buffs (although in some cases the old
part is the basement or back lean-to).

As of this writing, there are no motels in town; you'll find one
in Sandusky, fifteen miles inland. Golf addicts can take a swing
around the course just north of Port Sanilac.

The Port Sanilac harbor was built by the Army Engineers in the
fifties, has transient accommodations, fuel, tank pump-out, restrooms, and so forth. 313/622-8818. The boat launching ramp is
of limited depth; large craft may have trouble.

Small and rustic, this park has 112 acres, nineteen campsites, pit **PORT SANILAC**
toilets, a boat launch, and not much else except fine, clean sand **STATE PARK**
next to blue, blue water. And that's a lot.

Boat launch at Elk Creek, gravel-lined and shallow. **FORESTVILLE**

Public access. **HELENA ROAD**

Five miles south of Harbor Beach. Swimming, boating, nature study **WAGENER PARK**
area, ballfields, electricity, and forty-five campsites on M-25.

HARBOR BEACH • The largest town on the Lake Huron side of the Thumb. Once they had a beach but no harbor, so the citizens built (dug) what they claim is the largest man-made harbor in the nation. There is an Edison plant and some industry in town, but that doesn't mar the picturesque tranquility.

Frank Murphy (Detroit mayor, Michigan governor, Governor General of the Phillipines, Supreme Court Justice) was born in Harbor Beach. Murphy won a place in the heart of the labor movement when, as governor of the state, he refused to send the state troopers in to settle a Flint sit-down strike. A small museum on M-25 is full of Murphy mementos, and tours are conducted through his home. Call the number on the door if the museum is closed.

At **North Park** (M-25) there is picnicking, swimming, and camping spaces for forty-five units. There are four other parks nearby to bat a ball or bathe on the beach. Harbor Beach's docking area near mid-town has transient mooring, water, and electricity, but no repair facilities or supplies at the docks. Grocery and meat stores are about three blocks away. Boaters are warned that only shallow-draft craft can use the breakwater opening because of submerged cables.

Waterfront Festival Days are in mid-July.

PORT HOPE • The hamlet is almost invisible but the county runs a campground there with room for fifty-five trailers. That's Stafford Park.

LIGHTHOUSE PARK • Seven miles north on M-25, it has eighty-two campsites, swimming, and a large and pleasant spread. The lighthouse is privately owned but makes a great target for your camera. Small boat launch.

HURON CITY • A city in name only. What you'll find here instead is a collection of vintage buildings called the Pioneer Huron City Museum. It includes a "rescued" Coast Guard life-saving station with lifeboat and bell; a general store (a dandy!); a museum with two barns and a carriage shed, next to a boarding house and church. The museum focuses on Langdon Hubbard who founded the original town, and on William Lyons Phelps, an educator from Yale who made it famous.

Phelps was also a minister and he spent his summers preaching in the church, so successfully, in fact, that the congregation grew from 250 to 1000. The building was enlarged twice, and became a Sunday goal for the whole state. Phelp's house, Seven Gables, is closed to visitors but the rest opens during July and August. Small admission charged.

So named because of huge deposits of sandstone suitable for grind-stones ... an operation that ground to a halt years ago. Some huge round reminders rest forlornly along the shore. A neat little harbor park, one small private campground for trailers only, and fishing are today's offerings. The boat launching ramp is gravel-surfaced, suitable for small boats. • GRINDSTONE CITY

Pointe Aux Barque Road public access for small boats on ... • EAGLE BAY

Means "Point of Boats." The very tip of the Thumb is private property; the unusual rock cliff formations, seen from a boat, look a little like boats themselves. • POINTE AUX BARQUES

The friendly small town at the top of the Thumb has a harbor, a historical museum, and a drug store with a real soda fountain. You'll find a county park for swimming and boating. The long, wide pier offers the best shore fishing along the lake—according to those who inhabit it. Their buckets show the proof. • PORT AUSTIN

The harbor has transient facilities, fuel, dock attendant, haul-out and pump-out equipment. 517/738-8712.

Three miles southwest of Port Austin; eleven picnic tables on the water's edge. • ROADSIDE PARK

Picnic, swim, and row your boat. Seven miles from Port Austin on M-25. • MCGRAW PARK

Camping for seventy trailers plus all the above. Nine miles south-west of Port Austin on M-25. • OAK BEACH

The only campers-only park in the state park system. It has 665 acres, 181 campsites along a fine beach and water sports area. • PORT CRESCENT STATE PARK

49

SLEEPER ● Over 1,000 sunset-facing acres of trees, sand dunes, and beach;
STATE PARK 271 campers can enjoy modern facilities, but there's no boat launch
or park store. An understandably popular park.

You will notice as you continue driving on the Saginaw Bay
side of the Thumb that the motel and restaurant count has zoomed.
Bear these conditions in mind as you make your plans.

Much of the shore is in designated wildlife refuge areas, wetlands, and marshes—part of one of the state's favorite duck-hunt-
ing regions. Great migrations of birds flock to the bay, making it
a delight to wing-watchers and photographers. Want to catch Canada geese against the sunset? Here's the place.

CASEVILLE ● The harbor dock has accommodations for eight transients, gasoline, water, showers, and more. 517/856-4590. The county park
at Caseville welcomes about 200 campers as long as they don't
bring tents.

BAY PORT ● There are boat-launching sites in Bay Port with hard-surface ramps
that will handle all but the largest boats. The big event is August
Fish Sandwich Day. In a recent year 2,500 of the tasty combos
were sold in one day.

ROADSIDE PARK ● 2.5 miles south of Bay Port, with fourteen tables and grills in a
grove of hardwoods.

SEBEWAING ● Some very nice restaurants are nearby, where the talk is of fishing
or the next Sugar Festival, usually in July. The Luckhard Museum
preserves an old Indian mission, 660 E. Bay Street. Free. The boat
launch is on the Sebewaing River, next to the railroad bridge, near
the airport; it's concrete and has ample parking.

BAY PARK ● A boat launching site is at Belgian Drain. Good parking for a lot
of duck hunters or bird-migration watchers, but no camping.

QUANICASSEE ● Vanderbilt County Park; unimproved access site.

FINN ROAD ● Hampton Township launch ramp (no details available).

ESSEXVILLE ● A modest community with a picnic park but little along the water
except a boat launch at Burns Street off Woodside.

● BAY CITY

After Detroit, Bay City is the busiest Michigan seaway port on the
lakes, with a story revealing the best and worst of America's commercial history.

When Ben Pierce opened the first Bay City store in 1837 (the
same year Michigan became a state), the Saginaw Valley was thick
with forests, right up to the Saginaw River's edge. The combination
of a rich resource and easy transport soon turned Bay City into
the lumber capital of the world as an army of loggers and spec-
ulators sawed without restraint into the green-gold pie. By 1888
over four billion feet of lumber was taken out, enough to circle
the globe with a wide plank road. Lumber barons built their pal-
aces along Center Street until the axes had no more to chop.

The need to diversify industry was evident, and since those years
the city has become a leading producer of automobile parts, salt,
corrugated boxes, cheese, sugar, and electrical devices, to name a
few products. Ingenuity at its sharpest was demonstrated in World
War II when innovative building methods enabled shipyard workers
to turn out a navy vessel in a week.

Visitors can delve into more history at the Museum of the Great
Lakes, 1700 Center Avenue, near some of the homes mentioned.
Exhibits show glacial activity, fur traders, ship building, and period
rooms. A modest admission price; weekday hours are 10:00–5:00,
Sundays 1:00–5:00. 517/893-5733.

There's a lovely picnic area along the river (look for the East
Michigan Travel and Tourist Association's "Log Office" in Wenonah
Park and pick up more regional information) and a lot to see just
driving around downtown. For information contact Downtown
Bay City Inc., 401 Bay Bank Building, Bay City, Michigan 48706.
517/893-3573. Go to the neat old city hall and visit their bell
tower for an over-all view, or to the Chamber of Commerce, 205
Fourth Street. 517/893-1222.

The Brennan Marine showroom at 1809 S. Water is like a museum of modern boating; displays the largest power boat fleet in
outstate Michigan. Open 8:00–5:30 daily.

Boats can be launched at Veteran's Memorial Park.

Two nice events are the Summer Festival in mid-July, and the
Bay County Fair in early August.

BAY CITY STATE● On Saginaw Bay, M-247. The ratio of campsites (225) versus acreage
PARK (196) is not the best, but there is excellent fishing, a museum, a
park naturalist, and top facilities.

TREES — THE WATER WONDERLAND'S OTHER BLESSING

Green sentinels of the freshwater coasts, airy arches over inland streams
and picnic tables; habitat, crop, and place of beauty. More than half
of lucky Michigan is covered with trees.

The state stands in a wide zone between differing bands of climate
and vegetation. If you drive the length of I-75 (or the whole north-south
shore routes) you'll notice a shift in dominance from the needleleaf
conifers (evergreens) of the Canadian woods to the broadleaf decid-
uous (leaf-dropping) forests of the eastern United States. The vistas of
foliage include species common to both regions: oak, maple, birch,
aspen, spruce, fir, and pine.

Although most trees have a characteristic outline, they are easiest
to identify by their leaf, bark, flowers, and buds. There are a dozen
good tree guides on the market but I'll suggest the little volume put
out by Golden Books for beginning beginners partly because it fits so
well into pockets.

Here, in acorn-size summaries, are a few of the state's most common
varieties:

WHITE PINE Bearer of the official title "state tree," and once the back-
bone of the Michigan lumber industry, the white pine stands can be
seen in the northern lower peninsula (visit Hartwick Pines if you possibly can), but are more abundant in the Upper Peninsula. Blue-green
needles have five in a cluster; cones are long and narrow. Grows from
50 to 100 feet tall.

WHITE SPRUCE Important for its uses as pulpwood and saw lumber,
spruce is plentiful in the U.P. and northern lower peninsula. Each needle
is almost square in cross-section and they grow in rather tight spirals
around the twigs. The cones can be seen hanging down like Christmas
tree ornaments.

TAMARACK (LARCH) The evergreen that really isn't; its needles fall off
in the fall after turning yellow, grow back in tufts of ten or more. Much
used for poles and mine timbers, it's found mostly in the eastern Upper
Peninsula. Sometimes reaches more than 120 feet tall; Michigan average, 50 feet.

NORTHERN WHITE CEDAR (Arborvitae) Thick-packed and conelike, the leaves are flat with scales, and look as though they've been pressed into fans. Used a lot as an ornamental tree, the white cedar can grow to a height of 50 feet.

FIR Of some twenty-five species of fir trees, ten are found in the United States. All are thick and symetrical; the balsam is the most marvelously fragrant. Needles are flat on one side, grow right out of the twig without stalks, and leave little round scars when they drop off. Cones balance upright, perched as if they were sleeping birds. The Douglas firs of the West grow as high as 200 feet, but Michigan's tallest fir, the Scotch pine, quits at 70 feet.

MAPLE The big old friendly maple tree comes from a family of seventy or so species, a quarter of them North American. In Michigan the sugar, silver, and red maple are best known. Silver maple, rare north of Saginaw Bay, has deeply lobed leaves with whitish undersides; a shimmering spectacle when the wind blows, although not as bright as other maples during the fall color change.

Sugar maples (who needs to be told about maple syrup?) are the most important hardwood tree in the state, have shallow lobes, and turn a rich orange or red in the fall, while the red maple shows its reddish colors through the budding and leafing stages before getting super-red by fall. The red maples are a big lumber item in the U.P.

OAK A sturdy, spreading family with at least three dozen species in the eastern U.S. All oaks bear acorns which are quickly identifiable (as coming from oak trees) but their leaves show astonishing variety. Subdivided (mostly) into black and white oaks, Michigan grows four members of the "white" group: white oak, bur oak, swamp oak, and the uncommon chinkapin oak. White oak acorns mature in a single season and the leaves have rounded ends. Acorns of black oaks (northern red oak, pin oaks, and black oaks) take two seasons to ripen, and the trees have sharply pointed leaves.

BIRCH Yellow wonders of the autumn, three kinds of birch trees spread color through the northern woods: paper birch (canoe birch, white birch), recognized by its cream-white outer bark, a material Indians used for canoes and baskets; gray birch, which grows in thickets or clusters and has distinctly different leaves than paper birches; and yellow birch with a bark that peals in thin curly strips. The birch is one of the largest deciduous-leaved tree groups in the state.

BEECH Common low, bushy tree whose branches end in a flat-topped crown. Its broad, oval leaves have serrated edges, turn scarlet and orange in the fall.

ASPEN Abundant in the Upper Peninsula, the slender aspen is one of the first trees to grow in cut-over or burned-over land. Leaves come close to being round and shake nervously in the slightest breeze . . . hence the nickname "Quaking Aspen." Generally about 40 feet tall.

ASH The white ash, a member of the Olive family, likes to mix with Oaks and Maples, and is common throughout the state. Leaves are the "compound" kind: the seven to nine leaflets on a stem are really all one leaf. Branches soar upward to 80 or 90 feet.

NORTH TO CHEBOYGAN

TWELVE thousand years ago, when glacial ice was in retreat, "Lake Saginaw" projected its rounded contours halfway across the state and the low sand dunes of Midland County stood on the shore. Now the lake has become an enormous inlet of Lake Huron, its waters seeping into a low-level plain and transition zone of marshes, shallows, tall grasses, and calm ponds . . . vital habitat to fish and wildlife. Stacks of ecological studies have been done on the region as Michigan struggles with problems of coastal wetlands and waterfront abuse, public access and game protection.

No highway skims neatly along the waterworld of Saginaw Bay; even after you've rounded the bend at Au Gres, views of the bay are extremely rare. Sometimes it seems to take a bit more mileage than it should between glimpses.

The long blue edge beyond Tawas parallels a solidly sandy shore—with a bluff or two—until Alpena and the rugged outcroppings of Presque Isle, a favorite area for rockhounds.

Regions of the upper lake were once so thick with pine and spruce that settlement seemed impossible, yet towns grew steadily around the sawmills at the mouths of the logging creeks.

If you had investment capital in the 1870s, erecting a mill and chopping up the forest was a favored way of getting richer. Undaunted by fires and economic recessions, two thousand mills operated in the state in 1890, devouring the lumber crop like starving termites in an old shed.

The gluttonous consumption couldn't possibly last. When the

century turned, much of Michigan had a bleak, empty look; thoughtful citizens spurred a reverse action. An enormous tract spreading across much of the lower peninsula was set aside as the Huron National Forest, while Kiwanis clubs, Boy Scout troops, state bureaus, and civic groups began zealously planting millions of seedlings. Their combined efforts resulted in today's steady-yield forest and recreational haven.

Even discounting the sportsmen's ingrained policies of exaggeration, the fishing *is* good-to-excellent along the Huron streams, especially in the Au Sable. Scores of small lakes, hundreds of campsites, and miles of canoe streams dot and crisscross the Huron counties. Sometimes traffic is thick, but it's not a steady problem.

PARRISH ROAD● An unimproved access site, east off M-13 between Kawkawlin and Linwood.

LINWOOD— ● This 1,375-acre managed wildlife area, located at 1570 Tower
NAYANQUING POINT Beach Landing, sees up to ten thousand visiting ducks and geese
WILDLIFE CENTER each year. A stunning sight during the fall migrations, it's interesting any time. Three miles north of town, one mile east of M-13. Open 8:00 to 5:00, Mon.-Fri.

Area boat access site here, too.

PINCONNING ● Say cheese. Pinconning mild (and others) is their well-churned claim to fame, and a Cheese Festival is held every mid-July to celebrate (*mit* crackers).

For boaters there's a state access site off M-13, 3½ miles south, 2½ miles east on Coggins Road.

What are they catching out there? Northern pike, sunfish, channel catfish, and perch.

STANDISH ● M-13 blends into U.S. 23 and your route arcs toward the lake again. Just before town, off M-13 and east on Pine River Road, is an access site onto Wigwam Bay—a Saginaw Bay mini-inlet. Hard surface ramp.

ROADSIDE PARK ● Six miles northeast of Standish in a beautiful forest locale.

OMER ● U.S. 23 crosses the Rifle River, a ninety-mile stream that's a favorite with canoeists. Canoes and supplies are available in Omer and near the south Ogemaw County line.

A shore-to-shore hiking/biking/riding trail connects Lake Huron at Tawas to Lake Michigan. In midsummer 200 or so members of the Michigan Trail Riders Association walk their mounts out into the Huron surf then head west. It is advised to wait a while after this group departs before you start your own hike. **TAWAS CITY**

The East Tawas Harbor of Refuge has transient accommodations, gasoline, water, electricity, dock attendant, and pump-out. Call 517/362-2731. VHF-FM radio. Or write to Tawas Area Chamber of Commerce, 402 Lake Street, Tawas City, Michigan 48763. 517/362-8643.

On a land formation resembling a mini–Cape Cod, 202 camping units can enjoy 175 acres of trees and a two-mile beach. A wooden path (the Sandy Hook Nature Trail—complete with benches) over the dunes lets folks watch shore birds in action, passing sailboats, and the long ships on the far horizon. Groups who make careful advance requests may be allowed up into the lighthouse, otherwise it's just for cameras. Modern conveniences, boat launching ahead of the park entrance. **TAWAS POINT STATE PARK**

Another pair of twin communities. Oscoda is one of the largest, Au Sable one of the smallest townships in Michigan. The legend-loaded Au Sable River (trout, coho) flows into Lake Huron here, calling activities to the river banks as much as to the lake shore. Two "Queens," paddlewheel river boats, make trips to Cooke Dam, one starting from upstream, the other from Oscoda. Their schedule includes a cocktail cruise . . . and is especially delightful during fall colors. **AU SABLE–OSCODA**

The exciting and popular Au Sable River Canoe Marathon starts in Grayling and ends in Oscoda; late July.

A tall figure of Paul Bunyan reminds travelers that this is the northwoods superman's home. James MacGillivary, author of the Bunyan tales, was a native of Oscoda and is buried here. The annual Paul Bunyan Festival in midsummer lasts for days, and is filled with timberjack specialties such as log-rolling and chain saw exhibitions combined with a flea market, midway, and so forth.

Summer tours of nearby Wurtsmith Air Force Base are available through the Chamber of Commerce, plus fishing derby information.

As many as four boats at a time can be launched at the Oscoda facility at the mouth of the Au Sable. Fuel, parts, and service available.

Camping is possible at Van Ettan Lake Park and Old Orchard Park. For complete details write Oscoda–Au Sable Chamber of Commerce, 100 W. Michigan, Oscoda, Michigan 48750.

ROADSIDE PARK • Three miles north of Oscoda on Lake Huron.

HARRISVILLE STATE • No park store, boat launch, bathhouse, or refreshment stand, but
PARK   a beautiful place among stately pines and cedar. Ninety-four acres, 229 campsites right on the big lake.

HARRISVILLE • An Arts and Crafts Fair in August and the coastal August-September King Salmon Derby highlight summer life here, the site of another Harbor of Refuge. Transient accommodations, fuel, supplies, restrooms, showers, dock attendant, and more. 517/724-5242. VHF-FM radio.

STURGEON POINT • On county road east off U.S. 23, about four miles north of Harris-
LIGHT   ville. The lighthouse, built in 1869, has WW II airfield mesh bolting the door. Shipwrecks in the vicinity make the spot a favorite entering place for skin divers.

ALPENA • With a population of around 15,000, Alpena reigns as capital of the area, the largest city on the northern half of Huron's coast. In 1858 (which wasn't all that long ago) thirty settlers left their schooner behind and started buildng a town that today has a wildlife sanctuary within its limits, three city beaches, marinas, and a good supply of motels and restaurants.

The excellent Jesse Besser Museum is well worth a tour. A Gallery of Early Man displays the hardware and habits of early North Americans, and there are vehicles and equipment from the early white community. The Museum's art galleries have changing shows, there's a planetarium, and the grounds have added buildings: a pioneer cabin and an 1872 bank. Guided tours, lectures: 9:00–5:00 weekdays, Sat. 1:00–5:00, Sun. 7:00–9:00. 491 Johnson Street, Alpena, Michigan 49707 or call 517/356-2202.

East Tawas Point

Good fishing can be found on the floodwaters created by the power dams on Thunder Bay River; steelhead and brown trout, perch, and smallmouth bass are plentiful in the bay. For special doings come when the Alpena County Fair is on late in August, the Brown Trout Festival in late July, the Fourth of July sailboat races, or the late-July Art Show.

Alpena's Harbor of Refuge has room for transients, and all the services you could need. 517/354-5684. VHF-FM radio.

LONG LAKE • Camping for eighty, located eight miles north of Alpena on U.S. 23. Electricity, swimming.

PRESQUE ISLE • With a name that means "almost an island," this narrow peninsula has two lighthouses. The Old Presque Lighthouse was rumored to have been designed by Jefferson Davis, a legend research proves unlikely. Prize exhibits include a 3,425-pound bell, souvenirs from sunken ships, a weapons collection (blunderbusses, Samurai sword), and other antiques. You can go up in this lighthouse; after 140 steps you've got a beautiful view. Until Labor Day, 8:30 AM to 9:00 PM. A "new" lighthouse one mile north was built in 1870. No museum, just a pleasant walk around.

For both towers take county roads 405 or 638 east off U.S. 23, then follow the signs. These paths will also take you to two Lake Huron boat launching sites, one on Bell Bay near the southeast end of Grand Lake (the water that nearly turns Presque Isle into a real island), and the other at the north end of the lake at Grand Lake outlet, one mile off old State Road. For small boats only.

ROADSIDE PARK • U.S. 23, fronting on Grand Lake.

ROGERS CITY • A ship-conscious town that has known the deep tragedy of fathers and sons going down with their ships on the Great Lakes. The loss of the *Bradley* in 1958 and the *Cederville* in 1965—forty-three men in all—will come into the conversation if you visit long enough. Note the likeness of St. Ignatius Catholic Church to a ship.

Without a navigable river, Presque Isle County—where Rogers City serves as county seat—was late to develop. It was extremely isolated until the railroad came in 1911; an overland trip to De-

troit which took nearly two weeks, now can be covered in less than a day.

The world's largest limestone quarry is the basic factor in the economy. Limestone (along with the gypsum you saw in Alabaster) is vital in building materials, steel, chemicals, and other necessities. Watch them shovel and dynamite at "Quarry View," 9:00 AM to 5:00 PM, then hop over to the "Harbor View" where 1,500 freighters a year are loaded with rock. Road signs will tell you exactly where to go.

An easy twelve miles west of town off M-68 is Ocqueoc Falls, largest water drop in the lower peninsula. The campground has twelve sites, no swimming or boating, but good fishing in a lovely setting. Also of interest are the sinkholes in the southwestern corner of the county, spots where underground caves collapsed, leaving deep dents in the surface. The bottom of one is ninety feet lower than the surface of nearby Shoepac Lake. Camping for fifty plus a trail around the region. South of Onaway on Co. 35 then east on 634 to Perch Lake Road.

The Harbor of Refuge in Rogers City has room for a large number of transients, with fuel, pump-out, showers, dock attendant, and other services. 517/734-3808. (No radio as of this writing.)

Big Rogers City event is the Nautical City Festival, Lakeside Park, early August.

Sand dunes, foot trails, and more than a mile of superb beach. On 301 acres, the park has 144 campsites with everything except a camp store and boat launch. • HOEFT STATE PARK

Both tranquility and drama enfold this bluff forty miles from Mackinaw City. Stop to imagine being one of the voyageurs paddling westward, wondering if this could be the route to China. Or perhaps you're in one of the Chippewa's long canoes filled with beaver skins. The bluff is an old landmark. Not open to visitors, the $2\frac{1}{2}$-story lighthouse is surrounded by pleasantness that is open and breezy—a county park with picnic facilities but no camping. The boat access ramp will accommodate small trailerable craft only. • FORTY MILE POINT

HURON BEACH ● Roadside park.

HAMMOND BAY ● Harbor of Refuge with transient accommodations, fuel, water, showers, pump-out, dock attendant. 517/938-9291. VHF-FM radio.

ROADSIDE PARK ● Twenty-six miles beyond Rogers City, a scenic rest stop at Lake Huron sand dunes.

Note: Presque Isle county exemplifies Michigan's generosity to vacationers. There are two state parks and four forest campgrounds with more than 350 campsites. More than thirty roadside tables have been placed on U.S. 23 in this county alone.

ROADSIDE PARK ● Thirteen miles east of Cheboygan on the shore of Lake Huron.

CHEBOYGAN STATE ● A large park not fully developed, which makes it all the better for
PARK nature lovers. Swimming, camping for seventy-eight units on 932 acres.

CHEBOYGAN ● The name, an Indian word meaning "place of going through," is appropriate for the town linked via the Inland Waterway to Mullet Lake, Burt Lake, and forty-five miles of rivers, and eventually to Lake Michigan. (The route will handle any craft with a five-foot draft, and is well laid out with channel markers.) "Big Mac," the ice-breaking pride of the Coast Guard fleet, is moored in Cheboygan. Tours are available for summer visitors.

Go to jail, go directly to jail. . . . The odds-and-endsy historical museum once held the county rascals. On Huron and Court streets, open daily 1:00 to 3:00.

A brand new attraction is the boardwalk on the edge of the lake and over the cattail marsh. Fifty-four species of birds have been sighted flapping in and out of the tall reeds. Bring binoculars.

A daily scheduled mailboat will take you out to Bois Blanc (generally called Bob-Lo), where a small community gets along nicely on a mostly undeveloped island. Two golf courses are open to the public, two public marinas on the river serve boaters, and canoes and fishing craft are available to rent everywhere. Lots of motels and restaurants are here, in Mackinaw City, and in between.

Fishing derbies and contests crowd the summer calendar, but

you'll enjoy mushroom hunts in the spring, the 10,000-meter Road Race in June, and the Arts Festival in July, plus the Cheboygan to Bois Blanc Sail-in, and the Northern Michigan Open golf tournament in August. Cheboygan Chamber of Commerce, 616/ 723-2575.

● BOIS BLANC ISLAND

Don't worry about getting the right French accent—the name is "Bob-Lo," same as the amusement park in the Detroit River.

The ferries from Cheboygan and Mackinaw City land at Point Aux Pins, putting you in a pine-scented, 23,000-acre semiwilderness playground. There are motels, resorts, and little luxuries called restaurants and stores, but mostly Bois Blanc is a quiet place, dotted with half-a-dozen gleaming lakes—rustic living galore. . . .

If you leave your car in Cheboygan, a taxi can be rounded up to take you to and from the ferry landing or the airport . . . or even carry you to inland camping spots. Reservation advised.

The lighthouse on Lighthouse Point is an old-timer from 1857, the Michigan Waterways Department has a harbor here, and the Department of Natural Resources maintains a Bois Blanc field office.

For information contact the Cheboygan or Mackinaw City Chamber of Commerce.

● ALOHA STATE PARK

Just nine miles south of Cheboygan on Mullet Lake, this park has ninety-one acres and 284 campsites with a lovely sandy beach and choice fishing. No hiking trails or park naturalist, but all the comforts of home.

OUR DEBT TO THE GLACIERS

There were no Great Lakes before the glaciers—so how did it all happen? Between one and two million years ago (mere pittance in geologic time and nothing at all to a timeless Creator) the climate of North America changed drastically . . . not just once but again and again. Summers diminished to the vanishing point, snowfall increased, and great masses of ice piling up in the regions of Hudson Bay pushed slowly southward across the land.

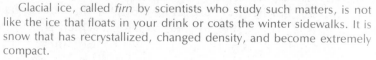

Glacial ice, called *firn* by scientists who study such matters, is not like the ice that floats in your drink or coats the winter sidewalks. It is snow that has recrystallized, changed density, and become extremely compact.

Well over a mile thick, these frigid canopies covered Michigan, reaching at one period from Missouri to New York and as far south as Kentucky. In a series of four "ice ages" (the Pleistocene Epoch), glaciers advanced and retreated, grinding, digging, and bulldozing the continental surface beneath their incredible weight. Just as a road grader spills a row of gravel along its blade edges or turns over boulders leaving holes and pits behind, the glaciers picked up debris (morain) from one spot and left it elsewhere, constructed long hills of rock and earth, and flattened others with their tremendous shoveling action. (Press your hand—fingers apart—into the surface of the beach, move it along and see the ridges and crests forming as you go.)

Warming periods lasted thousands of years, during which the probing fingers (lobes) of massive ice sheets melted into the troughs and basins their gouging and their enormous weight had produced. Wide lakes called Chicago, Duluth, Algonquin, and so forth appeared between glaciers and melt-offs . . . with only a faint resemblance to the present lakes.

Eventually, however, the last glacier receded and the long-depressed land (several localities sank as much as 3,000 feet beneath the pressure of the ice) rose slowly, draining some flooded areas and rearranging the contours of lakes and water sheds to their present form.

Time, erosion, and vegetation have dimmed the scars to near invisibility—unless you have the company of a geologist or good book on the subject to point them out. The exposed limestone bedrock on Kelly's Island in Lake Erie is one of the places where glacial grooves can be clearly seen. More obvious evidence is the shape of areas such as the northwest lower peninsula where the shoreline reflects the ins and outs of a glacier's "paw" and where a lengthy pile of glacial tailings was turned by large quantities of sand into the Sleeping Bear Dunes.

The *Atlas of Michigan* (Eerdmans Publishing Co.) condenses the glacial story with colorful stage-by-stage maps. For a more detailed account of glacial and other forces that have shaped our state, try *The Geology of Michigan* by Dorr and Eschmann (Univ. of Mich. Press).

MACKINAW CITY TO DRUMMOND ISLAND

Q UEEN of the Big Bend, Gateway to the Straits, Keeper of the
Lights, Guardian of the Ferries—all appropriate names.
Mackinaw City (notice that the name ends with an "*aw*" instead
of an "ac"; all "Mackinacs" are pronounced *aw*) straddles the
Emmet-Cheboygan County line and in reality touches the shores
of *two* Great Lakes, a neat geographic trick. Its heart and face
belong to Huron, however, and to the ferry boats pulling out
constantly for St. Ignace, Mackinac Island, or Bois Blanc.

Community roots go back to the building of Fort Michilimackinac and a first small settlement around a lighthouse. Growth came
with the boom of the lumber and fishing industries and death
nearly came with their decline. "Ghost town" seemed written into
Mackinaw City's fate ... until the rise of tourism. Its strategic
location has given the town more or less steady employment as
the number one traveler's aid station on the lakes. For years before
the bridge was built, local cooks catered to the motorists who
had to wait—sometimes for a day—to get their turn on the ferry
boat. Now people come up, some just to look at Big Mac or spend
a day at Mackinac Island, and find that Mackinaw City makes an
excellent base of operations. Motels are abundant and family restaurants fill the bill.

Down at the municipal marina the first craft in line is a brand
new replica of a 200-year-old armed sloop, the *Welcome*. Metic-
ulously hand-crafted, the vessel began as a Bicentennial project
based on authentic plans dug up from the archives of the British

Admiralty. For a small fee you can walk up the gangplank and inspect the hold.

The town is quite naturally full of bridge talk. Films, diving gear, wire spinners, cables, hard hats, newspaper clippings, and the small details of a big project can be seen at the Mackinac Bridge Museum (upstairs over a restaurant) on Central Avenue.

In Teysen's Talking Bear Museum, 416 South Huron Avenue, a detailed view of Indian daily life and art, food, herbs, pottery, and quill work is bound to teach and impress you. Also here are displays of blacksmithing, fishing, and logging days. Small admission, from mid-May until October, 9:00 AM to 9:00 PM.

The marina has transient accommodations, all the utilities, haul-out, pump-out, dock attendant. 616/436-5269. VHF-FM radio.

For more information, write to the Mackinaw City Chamber of Commerce, Mackinaw City, Michigan 49701. 616/436-5574. Ask about the Haunted Fort and the Mackinaw Music Show.

FORT MICHILIMACKINAC • Every Memorial Day weekend chattering crowds of visitors fill
STATE PARK specially erected bleachers to watch a strange ball game and remember a massacre. The spectators sit outside the stockade wall of the carefully restored fort while a cast of 200 citizens dressed as Indians, British troops, and French traders reenact a bloody bit of history.

The *why* behind the initial event has a lot to do with the differences in approach between the French and the British toward native Americans. The French (generally) learned their languages, copied Indian ways, and often became more Indian than French in the process. The proper British (and again generally) went by the book and applied military discipline to the "savages" who had trouble understanding how peace pacts made in places they never heard of could put their friends out and the stiff-necked newcomers in. Under the unifying leadership of Chief Pontiac an unprecedented number of tribes banded together and fought back, taking over all the British forts except Detroit.

Indian strategy at Michilimackinac was to lull and attack. A game of bagataway (lacrosse) did the lulling. Soldiers relaxed and watched; so did squaws ... but with hatchets hidden under their

The view from the Fort

blankets. When the ball went into the fort and the British opened the gates to let the players retrieve it, the Indians grabbed their hatchets and stormed in, slaughtering the hated Redcoats, wives and families included. French traders who happened to be within the fort weren't touched but had to watch, horrified and helpless.

Only one British officer, an old friend of an Ottawa chief, was spared, and he lived to write an eyewitness account for the history books.

The British eventually recovered, stayed another few years, then moved to a more strategic spot on Mackinac Island. As you tour the fort's chapel, officer's quarters, barracks, and blockhouses, the story of its stormy past is told with voices and dioramas.

A newer annual event is the Voyageurs Rendevous at the fort during Fourth of July festivities.

Reading material on forts and the bread-and-beans of frontier military life can be purchased at the Visitors Center, the unique building with the Mackinac Bridge for a roof.

The old Mackinac Point Lighthouse, part of the same complex, has been turned into a marine museum ... another tower you can't climb but which makes for good photographs.

No camping, only picnicking and bridge-watching, relaxing and learning. Operated by the Mackinac Island State Park Commission, open May to mid-October, daily 9:00 AM to 5:00 PM. Admission charged.

Note: The names of all these places, Mackinac or Mackinaw, originated with the word Michilimackinac. Generally translated "great turtle," some experts believe the true meaning is "great fault (or division) in the land."

THE MACKINAC • When you say "the world's most beautiful" about anything some-
BRIDGE one is going to argue that they know of a better specimen. However, the graceful cream and green span across the Straits of Mackinac is an artwork standing literally alone; an engineering wonder, an elegant path through space. No one debates the matter. No one has another bridge to compare it to.

From cable anchorage to cable anchorage, "Mighty Mac" is the world's longest suspension bridge, although the towers of the

The view from the top

Golden Gate Bridge and the Verranzano-Narrows Bridge are both higher and farther apart.

Bridge statistics can be fun. Michigan's five-mile-long champion weighs over a million tons, more than twelve Washington Monuments or 4,444 Statues of Liberty. 42,000 miles of wire are twisted into the supporting cables, 931,000 tons of concrete are poured into the road and substructure, 71,000 tons of steel give it strength. Nearly five million rivets hold the pieces together, every one present and accounted for ... and checked on regularly. The top of each tower is 522 feet above the water; people in cars are 199 feet high when they reach mid-span.

These numbers from a fact sheet tell little about the skeptics who said a bridge could *never* be built and the dreamers who built it anyway. Designed by David B. Steinman (who insisted on its colors), construction began in 1954 and was halted three times because of winter ice; the bridge was finally opened to traffic in November 1957. Before that date crossing was slow. The boat service had only a 462-car-per-hour capacity and sometimes the wait was half-a-day long. With the bridge, 6,000 cars can cross in a hour. Some poetic minds have dubbed this wondrous link the wedding band that "married" two peninsulas.

You'll need only ten minutes to make the drive, a passage that *cannot* be interrupted with a pause to take pictures. Those who have trouble with heights may be reassured to know that "freezing" is not uncommon. The bridge personnel will come to your assistance.

Love of the Mackinac Bridge has inspired a congenial, low-keyed but high-pitched athletic event every Labor Day. The only

BRIDGE FARES

Car (including all passengers)	$1.50
Car with 1 axle trailer or coach	2.50
Car with 2 axle trailer or coach and buses	3.50
Motorcycle	1.00

Bicycles must be transported. Inquire.
For more information: St. Ignace Chamber of Commerce, 48933. 906/643-8717.

time in the year when pedestrians are allowed, on this day Michigan citizens come by the thousands (between twenty-five and thirty thousand) to amble, saunter, and stride up and over "their" bridge. Walkers must start from the St. Ignace side (north) between 7:30 AM and 10:00 AM on the day of the one-way-only walk. All bikes, roller skates, unicycles, and pets are to be left behind. Only small wagons or strollers for the little tots are allowed ... and everyone is warned to use the plumbing before starting out. The big walk costs nothing, but you need fifty cents for the bus ride back to the north side and your car. Bridge walkers are a determined lot and come in all ages, eight months to eighty. Everyone gets a certificate upon reaching the finish line. If you'd like to join, remember: 10:00 AM is the absolute deadline; people have been known to drive for twelve hours, arrive at 10:05 and find the barricades up.

No boat launch or bathhouse, but a grand view of *the* bridge for ● STRAITS STATE PARK 181 camping units. Immediately east of I-75. Adjoining the west side of the bridge approach is the Father Marquette Memorial and National Historic Site, a must-visit for everyone. A circular stone wall with a curved beam "roof" soars upward: not a chapel, not a shrine, but a fittingly simple, powerful tribute. A few steps away is the Father Marquette Museum, a modern beauty with well-appointed theater and displays on the life of the man who founded St. Ignace and Sault Ste. Marie, discovered and mapped the Mississippi, and much more. Beautiful viewing spot.

Open spring through fall, 8:00 AM to 8:30 PM. Admittance to Marquette Unit of Straits State Park is by Park motor vehicle permit. There is no additional entrance fee for the museum.

Call 906/643-8620 or write Straits State Park, St. Ignace, Michigan 49781.

This community's first beginning came when Pere Jacques Mar- ● ST. IGNACE quette led a band of 200 converted Huron Indians to the shores of this Upper Peninsula bay and established a mission in 1671, naming it after St. Ignatius Loyola, founder of Marquette's Jesuit order.

St. Ignace's story is not one of steady growth from that moment on. The location was abandoned at least once, but a permanent settlement was bound to come; the bay was too handy to Mackinac Island, too accessible to lower Michigan, too filled with fish, and just too pretty not to move toward being a sizable community. In 1882 it became the seat of Mackinac County, a year before the first telegraph cable was laid across the Straits. St. Ignace's first movie was shown in 1907; it was the last city in Michigan where you just picked up the receiver and told Tillie the operator what number you wanted. In 1971 St. Ignace celebrated its 300th birthday.

The Michilimackinac Historical Society Museum on Spring Street features a dozen permanent exhibits on lumbering, Great Lakes shipwrecks, Upper Peninsula history, and Chief Wawatam, an Indian hero. Open daily in June, 11:00 AM to 5:00 PM, July and August weekdays and Sat., 1:00–5:00. Donation. 906/643-9570.

Another spot to browse through the past is the Fort de Buade Museum, on the site of an old stockade and full of antique Indian beadwork, guns, and French and British relics. You can see—but you wouldn't want to paddle—a genuine 300-year-old dugout canoe. 334 N. State Street, open May 29 till Labor Day, seven days a week, 9:00–9:00. 906/643-8686.

The Frontier Museum and the Treasure Island Museum, on the same waterfront thoroughfare, have even more to see.

State Street, alias business loop I-75, coils around the little inlet and manages to look frontierish, even in these days. In June the big event is the Straits Antique Auto Show on Dock #2. A bright Fourth of July is the midsummer gala, and the Black Gown Tree Pageant, dramatizing the life of Father Marquette, is played without cost to Labor Day–weekend audiences right at the water's edge.

Motels and restaurants are the main business (after museums and ferry boats) of St. Ignace; simple cabins or luxury rooms, pancake parlors or cocktails and cutlets.

Local sight-seeing is not complete without going to Castle Rock, just north on I-75, and climbing the unmentioned number of steps

to the top. It costs twenty-five cents, but on a clear day the view is well worth it.

Ferries leave for Mackinac Island every half hour during July and August; slightly reduced schedules apply in May-June and September-October. The trip takes about thirty minutes, costs (subject to change) $4.50 for adults, $3.00 for youngsters four to twelve.

St. Ignace Harbor facilities include transient accommodations, fuel, restrooms, tank pump-out, dock attendant. VHF-FM radio, telephone. 906/643-8131.

In an old movie about the doomed Titanic, Clifton Webb—playing the eternal snob—sneered at Barbara Stanwyck for being from a place called Mackinac. To an English socialite, Mackinac sounded like the boondocks. Once you've been to Mackinac Island, however, everywhere *else* seems rock-bottom. This green crown topping the northern waters of Lake Huron is Michigan's ivory tower, our enchanted attic, our version of Camelot.

MACKINAC ISLAND

Mackinac Island

Ferry passengers first see luxury cottages and the Grand Hotel with its famed 880-foot porch gleaming over the treetops as they approach the island; then they enter a harbor picturesque enough to be straight off a Disneyland drawing board. Shining white Fort Mackinac sits up on a bluff like part of a stage setting; Victorian storefronts, old but dapper hotels with porches full of rocking chairs, a forest of sailboat masts, a white church steeple, horses and buggies, people on bikes. . . .

The nineteenth century dominates the look and tempo of twentieth-century Mackinac Island the way college years dominate whole life-times. No cars are allowed, no glassy, cantilevered modern structures hit the eye. You know the machinery of modern life is there but not even the sight of TV antennaes or carriage drivers responding into their walkie-talkies can mar the sense of a time warp.

The Chippewas claim the island was Eden, created first, and the Great Spirit was so pleased with his effort that (after taking time to form the rest of the world) he came back to Mackinac to live. Their tribes had powwows here; they buried their dead in island caves. Then the first French voyageur paddled past in his canoe and nothing was ever the same.

Two forces were soon at work. Zealous missionaries came to find converts and often martyrdom, and a rough breed of adventurous woodsman came to find furs. The pelt of the beaver was as good as gold, thanks to the demand for furs by the aristocrats of Europe. Into an unbelievably lucrative business (thought for years by the French to be their permanent monopoly) stepped John Jacob Astor, whose American Fur Company was a business phenomenon. Astor's Mackinac Island warehouse and office are now museums.

The political history of Mackinac is best told by guides at the fort or docents at the museums. After several switches of command the island became American territory and its story shifted into another gear.

In the same way that lumbering died out later, the fur trade died of its own excesses, and by the mid-1800s Mackinac had turned to fishing. For years enormous hauls of whitefish and trout were barreled and shipped daily, keeping a fleet of fifty schooners busy ... but even that was not to last. Another, even more profitable business, was rising to replace it: tourism.

As the island became more popular, word began to spread. William Cullen Bryant once declared, "... the manifest destiny of Mackinac Island is to be a watering place ... there is no air more pure and elastic...." "It is so healthy here," quipped a soldier in 1830, "that a person has to get off the island to die."

These word-of-mouth reviews had a strong effect. The Protestant mission building was purchased and converted to a hotel in 1852, and more soon followed. Wealthy passengers on the new luxury steamboats demanded the best; Mackinac Island gave it to them and became *the* place to summer.

In 1875, the isle was the second place (after Yellowstone) to be declared a national park. Twenty years later the park was turned over to Michigan, owner of eighty-six percent of its five-square-mile surface.

U.S. Senator F. B. Stockbridge shrewdly bought some acreage in 1882, persuaded cronies like Cornelius Vanderbilt that the best could be even better, and set out to build the grandest hotel the world had ever seen ... *immediately*. Money works. The Grand Hotel was erected in ten months even though construction had to continue through a severe winter with supplies hauled by sled across the ice.

That was 1886 and the hotel, still a world leader today, recently "starred" in the movie *Somewhere in Time*. Presidents, tycoons, and traveling potentates are on the guest register. Visiting the Grand is part of what you do at Mackinac (but don't try to enter the lobby in beachwear), along with stopping at historic houses, buying fudge, or taking a seven-mile swing around the island on a rented bike.

The Indian dormitory, Mission Church Museum, St. Anne's Church, Dr. Beaumont's home (he made medical history by studying a man's stomach through a wound that wouldn't close), and a natural arch rock formation are all on the points-of-interest list.

A golf course is open to the public, and Fort Mackinac has historic exhibits plus frequent demonstrations of muzzle-loading on its neat parade ground.

A brand-new island attraction is the horse and carriage museum, starring cutters and surreys used by filmmakers when Hollywood chose Mackinac Island as a background. The sleigh used by Spencer Tracey and Katherine Hepburn in *Sea of Grass* and the 1980 buggy in which Christopher Reeve and Jane Seymour rode in *Somewhere in Time* are on display. Run by Mackinac Island Carriage Tours, the museum is free.

No camping is allowed on Mackinac, but there's a lot of grand hiking through the woods on the nearly-empty northern section of the island.

The lilac-loving French planted the first bushes and now the blooming of more than fifty varieties signals a big Lilac Festival in mid-June, a season opener. The popular Chicago to Mackinac and

Les Cheneaux Island

Port Huron to Mackinac yacht races in July keep all six hotels booked far in advance and the lake filled with small craft watching the finishers come in.

For hotel, tour, Fort information write or call: Mackinac Island Chamber of Commerce, Mackinac Island, Michigan 49757. 906/847-3783.

Now that you've had your Mackinac Island fudge fix, climbed Castle Rock, and had your picture taken in front of the Paul Bunyan statue, head for the M-134 exit off I-75 and Les Cheneaux (Lay She-no, sometimes called The Snows) Island territory.

BAY CITY LAKE CAMPGROUND

Three miles north and slightly west of Hessel via Three Mile Road. Twelve campsites, swimming, fishing, and a path through some old sand dunes are offered by this State Forest spot.

The small Hessel airfield sits just east across the paved road.

HESSEL

A Harbor of Refuge site, Hessel offers the first chance to launch a boat into the islands. Fuel, electricity, showers, haul-out facilities, dock attendant, and pay station phone are available.

Come in early August to watch the annual antique boat show and regatta, a rare kind of gathering. Boats of every description sail or putt-putt into the harbor, their vintage hulls and brass deck cleats glistening like tomorrow. Arts and crafts, dancing, and more make it Hessel's biggest day of the year. The Les Cheneaux Chamber of Commerce will give exact dates and details: Cedarville, Michigan 49719. 906/484-3935.

CEDARVILLE

A site known to the voyageurs, named for the enormous quantity of cedar posts and railroad ties shipped from its harbor. The Cedarville Historical Museum, housed in a genuine settler's log cabin, is open from June 1 to Labor Day and has a good bit to say about Cedarville's early struggles.

A supply of motels and resorts makes this your best bet for finding room if you plan to explore locals woods and waters. Call ahead, however.

Thirty-six islands, like wooded stepping stones (Paul Bunyan size) hug the north Lake Huron shore. Only one of them—Government Island—is public land. If you have a boat there's a campground and picnic site on the island's north end.

Cedarville's harbor has a boat launch ramp plus public docking. Big all-out event is the Fourth of July celebration. For more information, write to the Chamber of Commerce (see address under **Hessel**).

DETOUR STATE PARK • An undeveloped park with high wilderness appeal. Pit toilets and hand pumps. A very good beach (the park brochure calls the water temperature "moderate"; believe *cold*). Rocky stretches are great for mineral collectors; fishing for perch and bass is generally productive. There's lots of privacy, with twenty-two campsites on 407 acres. Camp registry is the honor system, but rangers from Straits State Park make frequent checks.

DRUMMOND ISLAND • It's bad enough to lock the barn door after the horse has been stolen, but imagine the chagrin of Sir Gordon Drummond, British commander of the "Lakes District" in the very early 1800s. Sir Gordon either didn't know or didn't care that the Americans were granted Drummond Island after winning the Revolution, and that the deed was even more securely cemented after the War of 1812. Drummond, apparently not one to listen to rumors, built a fort on what was the enemy's soil. Not until the late date of 1822 did he finally abandon everything and get over to Canadian territory.

What scant traces are left of Drummond's debacle occupies private property now, but his name remains to grace the Upper Peninsula's largest Lake Huron island, covering 136 square miles and including forty inland lakes.

The frequent ferries from DeTour don't land near the main settlement—they just set you on the road toward it. A "Welcome to Drummond Island" gateway, built to resemble a frontier stockade, has been painted as brightly as a coral red barn; a rare splash of hot color in this cool blue green outpost.

The village of Drummond spreads along a mile and a half of roadway, offers a couple of restaurants and coffee shops, places to buy groceries, and the Drummond Island Museum, open on summer afternoons.

Although most people come by car or on their own watercraft, Drummond Island has a sod landing strip for private planes ... which makes for an unusual golf hazard. Golf course and airport, you see, occupy the same stretch of meadow, with five holes on one side of the runway and four holes on the other. It is uncertain whether the pilots yell "fore!" or the golfers *whirr* loudly.

If you're a rockhound and would like to see the inside workings of the world's largest dolmite quarry, that can be arranged via the Drummond Dolmite Company office.

No municipal marina here, but there's a yacht haven that will be glad to service your boat. For information regarding resorts, motels, housekeeping cabins, and so forth, write to the Chamber of Commerce, Drummond, Michigan 49726. 906/493-5245.

DeTOUR VILLAGE TO SAULT STE. MARIE

THE island-strewn passage between Lakes Huron and Superior is *in toto* the St. Mary's River, although it widens into bays and lakes, and thins into narrow channels. Potagannissing Bay lies on the north side of Drummond Island; Munuscong Lake, the Neebish and Munuscong channels, and Lake Nicolet are beyond that. Then the bubbling St. Mary's rounds a bend, rushing twenty-one feet downhill toward the south in swift and swirling currents. Until the building of the locks not even the lightest Indian canoe could make it upstream against this flow. Everything was portaged.

The lands along the St. Mary's gleaming pathway have a low population density and are generally what the outdoor person's dreams are made of: good fishing, plenty of elbow room, few motels, and fewer restaurants. You can get supplies at DeTour or Goetzville, but it is best to come equipped.

The ferry between DeTour and Drummond Island cuts across shipping lanes of traffic headed for Duluth or points south. From DeTour to Neebish the shore is sandy, at times rocky, but not always easy to reach—there's no road along the edge, no parks or scenic turnouts. Bass, perch, and pike are the fish to go after.

Farther up, the Munuscong River State Forest offers a campground with fifty sites and excellent fishing. Under the watchful eye of the Munuscong Waterfowl Management Unit, 465 acres of nearby wetlands are designated waterfowl refuges, a marvelous spot for bird watchers and photographers.

Close to a Coast Guard station and the tiny community of Nee-

bish, you can catch a ferry to Neebish Island, one of the three large islands in the river belonging to the United States. An access site is two miles north of the ferry dock at the south end of Lake Nicolet. The main county road north gets close to the lake at Harmony Beach and will take you right around to downtown, locks and all. At Sault Ste. Marie's city limits, a municipal marina and boat launching site may be what you're looking for.

●NEEBISH ISLAND

About seven miles long and four miles wide, Neebish shows up as Nibish or Aneebish on some old maps. Two theories are promoted about the name: that it is a word for "grand foliage" *or* "where the river boils." Whatever, Neebish is a popular goal for fishermen and duck hunters.

●SUGAR ISLAND

Long, angular "Sisibakwatominiss," Chippewa for "Maple Sugar Island," *does* have a lot of maple trees, which put on a splendid show in the fall. When the British were still around they called it St. George's Island and—like Drummond—gave it up with great reluctance. In fact, ownership wasn't definitely settled until 1842. A gravel boat launch ramp can be found on the St. Mary's River, the northeast corner of the island, suitable for medium and small boats.

On the near side (right across from Sault Ste. Marie) the big freighters come within 300 feet of the shore; a good place for a wide-angle lens.

Note: Neebish and Sugar islands have almost no public lands. Please observe property rights and laws.

81

BEACH BIRDS, SWAMP SINGERS, POND PADDLERS, and A FEW OTHERS . . .

If one single sound—beyond the breaking of a wave upon the beach—signifies "shore," it is the raucous but somehow cheerful call of the gull. Without those graceful aerialists hovering in the wind, skiing down their invisible hills, and endlessly scolding each other, the whole waterfront setting is an unfinished scene. So is a marsh without the chirp of the redwing; or the woods without owls and warblers.

Estimates of the world bird population have run as high as 100 billion. A rough guess puts the U.S. bird count at 5½ billion and Michigan's seasonal peak runs into many millions. All these individual birds classify into 8,580 known species around the world; 300 species can be spotted in Michigan.

That's a lot to keep track of, but the state is also full of hawk-eyed bird-watchers, Audubon societies, nature centers, wildlife refuges, etc.; people who count and band birds, write books and pamphlets, raise funds for sanctuaries, and otherwise promote featherhood.

With such ready help, now is the time to tune out your radio and tune into birds. Don't travel without a pair of binoculars and a bird guide in your glove compartment. Tag after the park rangers; listen to the voices in the trees. Those chirpers are our number-one ally in insect control, our early-warning system on the state of the environment.

The list that follows may be as short as a robin's tail, but perhaps it will serve as a beginning. The birds included are ones you are most apt to see while traveling the coast . . . plus a couple you will be *very* lucky to glimpse in a lifetime.

COMMON TERN "Sea gull," "sea swallow," . . . "Jonathon Livingston Tern"? The common tern is smaller than a gull but quickly recognized by its black-tipped coral beak, black cap, forked tail, and slender wings. They nest in colonies amid the beach grass; lay olive grey or beige spotted eggs, three or four at a time.

RING-BILLED TERN A grey-white scavenger that follows ships and farmer's plows, hoping to find dead fish or turned-up worms. Along with the distinctive stripe on their beaks, ring-bills have a dark, clearly marked tail.

CASPIAN TERN Small feathers at the back give the Caspian's head a slightly different shape, and his bright beak has no black tip. Not much of a nest-builder, the Caspian scratches a hollow near the beach grass, throws in a few leaves, and lays two or three eggs.

HERRING GULL The bigger cousin of the tern (they hold family reunions in the wakes of ships), herring gulls are also scavengers. Black wingtips, pink legs, white head and underbody, pearl-grey back. The young gull is a conservative shade of brown, takes three years to grow into his adult outfit.

SPOTTED SANDPIPER Teetering clownishly up and down as it walks, the sandpiper is one of the most common shore birds, one of the easiest to identify. Brown back, clearly spotted breast. The nest is close to the ground, hidden under brush, and apt to contain four creamy-white, brown-speckled eggs.

CANADA GOOSE Like the whistle of a steam train twisting through a valley, the honking of Canada geese in their long V-shaped flight patterns against the fall or early spring sky imprints one's memory forever. Long black necks, white throat patches and sheer size make them easy to recognize. Canada geese eat a few insects but prefer plants, lay five to eight dull greenish or beige eggs at a time. Usually Canada geese mate for life.

COMMON LOON Dressed in a fancy outfit of checkered black and white with a white bib, the loon is one of the state's largest diving birds, can take the plunge and swim long distances underwater. Nests are always built very close to the water since loons are not much on walking around. Their call is a bit like a yodel; eggs are rather dark green and scarce . . . only two are laid at a nesting.

MALLARD DUCK Large, common mallards are picturesque ducks; "Ma" mallards and ducklings have inspired story books, and their way of crossing roads from pond to pond have stopped more than one lane of traffic. The green head and white neck ring of the more colorful males are easy to spot. They feed on aquatic plants in shallow water but also go for grain in fields with no pond or lake around. It's good that there are a lot of them; mallards make excellent eating.

CANVASBACK Another large, delicious bird, the canvasback has a rust-colored head, black breast, and long, sloping profile. Swims low in the water, dives in a flash, and lays nearly a dozen green-gray eggs at a time.

WOOD DUCK A crown of feathers gives the appearance of being combed back, an arrangement that inspired teen-age hairdos a while ago. Males have a bright reddish area on their bills, females wear a mask of white around their eyes. Just as the name implies, they like

BIRDS IN BUNCHES

Our language has developed special terms for special bird groups. Examples:

- a gaggle of geese
- a sord of mallards
- a seige of herons
- a plump of wildfowl
- a cast of hawks
- a bevy of quail
- a brood of chickens
- a covert of coots
- a host of sparrows
- a walk of snipe
- an exaltation of larks
- a murmuration of starlings
- a badelyng of ducks

the streams and small ponds of the forests and make their nests in trees that branch out over the water. When it's time for the young 'uns to leave home they simply fall to the water and swim away. Completely protected by law.

COMMON MERGANSER Loonlike birds, mergansers seem to specialize in long, half-running take-offs and wide-winged "skidding" landings. Black heads and wingtips, white necks and breasts, the favorite meal is small fish, and choice nesting spots are tree cavities. Six to sixteen creamy beige eggs.

AMERICAN BITTERN Unless you're really sharp you may not spot this timid member of the heron family who lives in marshes and "freezes" into a brown oval with his beak pointing up whenever someone comes near . . . thus looking for all the world like a bent cattail. The bittern dines on frogs, builds platform-like nests, and lays half-a-dozen eggs.

SANDHILL CRANE The tallest bird in the state and certainly one of the most spectacular, you may get a chance to spot one around the Seney Wildlife Refuge or in the bird sanctuaries of the mid-southern lower peninsula. Even though the flying crane is clearly not a goose (cranes fly with their feet extending behind their tails), hunters are among the menaces sandhills face. Two eggs hatch at a time from the large, remote nests, and the young aren't ready to fly for nearly a year.

GREEN HERON Seems to be wearing bright yellow stockings and black feathers, but when you get closer to this common, smallish bird it's definitely green. If you see it flying by you might think it's a crow. The feathers on its head go up when alarmed or its dinner of fish and insects is interupted. Three to six pale blue eggs make up the annual nest.

REDWINGED BLACKBIRD Easily spotted in nearly every marsh you'll come to, the male wears red and yellow patches on his wings, the female is a conservative brown. Their meals are insects and weed seeds; eggs are white with brown streaks. The song of the red-wing (how can "o-caa-lee" on paper convey anything musical?) is bright and cheering. Listen a while.

BELTED KINGFISHER Where there are fish to be caught, there are long-beaked, crested kingfishers to catch them. Head feathers give a distinctive Bohemian appearance; white collar, blue-gray feathers, and a harsh, raspy call add to the image. They build their nests in tunnels dug into the river bank and average about seven eggs, all creamy white.

GREAT BLUE HERON How such large birds get by on such long skinny legs is something to wonder at, but the blue heron—a vision of precise balance—can be seen stepping slowly and daintily through the marshes and wooded swamps. Dark feathers bouce airily behind their heads; the rest of their bodies are slate blue, except for a pinkish neck. Unlike cranes, herons pull their necks back into their shoulders in flight. Shy and wary, they build bulky nests, drop four or five bluish eggs.

GREAT HORNED OWL A powerful, aggressive resident of the deep forest with feathers sticking up exactly like horns. Mostly brown with yellow eyes and a white necktie, its sharp beak and talons makes short work of rats and gophers. Not much of a nest-maker, the horned owl beds down in the nearest old crow's nest or finds a place in a hollow tree and lays two or three white eggs. The Barred Owl gives eight hoots, the Spotted Owl three or four, and the Horned Owl repeats his call five to seven times. Nice to know as you burrow down in your sleeping bag.

RAVEN Big brother to the crow, the huge black birds are a common sight in the Upper Peninsula, especially in the Marquette and Keweenaw areas. Pairs of birds use the same nest for years, making annual repairs when needed. Its five or six eggs are elongated ovals, aqua with brown splotches. All they ever quoth is "Caw!"

BALD EAGLE At one time these great winged national emblems were plentiful, but many were killed by fishermen who saw them as rivals, or by sheep raisers who felt they were a threat to the flocks. Eagles are also threatened by pesticides which have caused infertility. As fish is the eagle's favorite food, their nests (which are the size of upside-down beaver dams) are usually in tall trees or cliff edges near water. The same nest will last for years and their mating is for life. Two or three large white eggs are laid; both parents feed the young.

YELLOW WARBLER Even non–bird-watchers have noticed this bright singer flitting around in low bushes and thickets near streams. Plentiful and easily observed, the yellow warbler is found throughout the state, and has a tiny compact nest that could almost be glazed and used for a teacup. The cowbird makes life hard for warblers by muscling in on their territory, but the yellow birds get even by covering up the cowbird's eggs, thus preventing them from developing. When they lay their own, four or five bluish eggs are average.

MUTE SWANS "Swans can swim while sitting down, for pure conceit they take the crown . . ." wrote Ogden Nash. All small ducks are supposed to want to be swans—the beauty queens of the lake—when they grow up, since swans are the largest members of the duck family, Anatidae. The big, graceful creatures eat mostly aquatic plants, and nest in masses of vegetation on little islands or marshy banks. In migration or at their winter retreats swans will mingle with other birds, but in their home breeding grounds they pair off exclusively, can inflict real harm on birds or humans who come too near. The male is a cob, the female a pen, and the young are cygnets. Only the language experts know why.

ROBINS The state bird, a cheery harbinger of spring—even the shortest list of Michigan birds has to include robins. A few of them stay around all year, but most robins decide warm weather is better and head south. Nests are built in early spring in trees, porches, on the jutting edges of buildings. The female lays four or five blue-green eggs, incubates them, and both parents keep the youngsters fed for the next two weeks. When the kids are fully on their own the parents start another family.

KIRTLAND'S WARBLER A bright little songbird that has won national fame because of the fight for its preservation. Conditions have to be just so—only a limited sixty-square-mile area in Michigan's lower peninsula will do: the jack pine where the nest is built can't be taller than fifteen feet or shorter than five feet. Fussy. However, the number of nesting pairs is slowly going up from a low of 167, and it is hoped that before long a goal of 1,000 nesting pairs will be reached, a number considered necessary for keeping the species alive and well.

Sassy tern

PART THREE

LAKE MICHIGAN

MICHIANA TO POINT BETSIE; SLEEPING BEAR TO
WILDERNESS STATE PARK; WESTWARD TO MENOMINEE

LAKE MICHIGAN STATISTICS

Length	307 miles
Breadth	118 miles
Length of coastline excluding islands	1,400 miles
Total water surface	22,300 square miles
Drainage basin	45,600 square miles
Maximum depth	923 feet
Volume of water	1,180 cubic miles

LAKE MICHIGAN

O N a plane to Chicago, a young man was making his first flight over any of the Great Lakes. "We've just gone past the shoreline—but where's the other side?" He concentrated for several long minutes, waiting for the far side to show up, and finally exclaimed, "We're *still* not across!"

The size of these great sprawling waters continues to amaze us, but the scope of what they touch is just as astounding. Lake Michigan is the only one of the Great Lakes entirely within the boundaries of the United States; its the fifth largest lake in the world. From some of the world's tallest buildings to pup tents in the north woods, every phase of America's growth and economy, every ethnic group and cast of mind, is represented in the twenty million people and their various works along the Lake Michigan coast.

Jean Nicolet was the first to paddle a canoe into the lake, but it was Jacques Marquette and Louis Jolliet who brought some sense of definition, a mapable experience, to the knowledge of the continent. It was all done on direct orders from the "Sun King," Louis XIV, to explore "his" territory. The French had planted themselves at Sault Ste. Marie and gallishly proclaimed everything from the Soo westward to the next ocean (they had no idea where *that* could be) as belonging to His Royal Majesty ... a rather classic example of arrogance and ignorance. Marquette and Joliet were to be relieved of their mission posts long enough to do some exploring, an edict the adventurous priests eagerly obeyed. Together they paddled along the north shore of the lake to Green

Bay, then followed the Fox River through the land of the Illini toward the Mississippi, returning via the site of Chicago and up Michigan's western edge.

Clearly this was a much larger continent than even the king of France could imagine!

The darkly wooded shores, unmarked hazards, and scarcity of food marking the first journey make today's traveler seem like a fairly coddled egg. However, there are still opportunities for adventure. Diving to sunken ships, for example, is a growing sport that involves history, risk, and delving into tragic records.

Beginning with the mysterious disappearance of the *Griffin*, the first sailing vessel on the lakes, to the sinking of the *Bradley* in 1958 (a limestone carrier with a crew of thirty-eight), Lake Michigan has taken a grim toll. As with all the Great Lakes, its storms are not to be underestimated, although the greatest single disaster was the capsizing of the excursion steamer *Eastland* within grasp of the Chicago docks in 1915. Eight hundred fifteen people died under the overturned boat.

While the wet-suit crowd searches the depths, strange new birds are flying overhead. Hang gliding, nicely fostered by Ma Nature who provided high dunes, soft landing spots, and favorable air currents, can be watched and practiced in a dozen places along Michigan's shore.

Thousands of sailboats heel to the wind every summer, silently passing thousands of motorboats filled with intent practitioners of the still favorite sport of fishing. Steelhead, salmon, trout, and coho head the list. During the height of the coho runs the fishermen are thicker than marsh grass along the banks of the feeder streams, and few quit to go home early. If this appeals, the West Michigan Tourist Association (listed in back of the book) will tell you where to rent a boat, find a motel, and other essentials.

Lake Michigan's wide waters help to moderate the climate of the western edge of the state, tempering the Arctic blasts coming across the plains ... making conditions right for fruit growers. A third of the world's cherries come from the Traverse City area, but vineyards, apple orchards, blueberry patches, and more provide the stock for pie factories, wineries, and roadside stands all along the lake. In the Department of Agriculture's guide *Country Carousel* (to obtain a free copy, write to Department of Agriculture, Lansing, Michigan 48909), Berrien County in the southwest corner of the state is named the leader for farms with special you-pick bargains.

WHAT'S THE KETCH?

Masts and sails together are referred to as rigs. Rigs with four-sided sails are gaff-headed rigs; rigs with triangular sails are jib-headed. Single-masted vessels (by far the most numerous) are called sloops, but variations on the one-mast theme include catamarans, cutters, sailing dinghies, etc.

A sail-watcher's notebook

When there are *two* masts, you are looking at a yawl, ketch, or schooner. Placement of the two masts makes the difference, whether the tallest (mainmast) is in front or behind the shorter mast. When the shorter mast is in front it's the *foremast*; when it's in back of the mainmast it's called the *mizzenmast*.

Confused? Maybe this mini-chart will help:

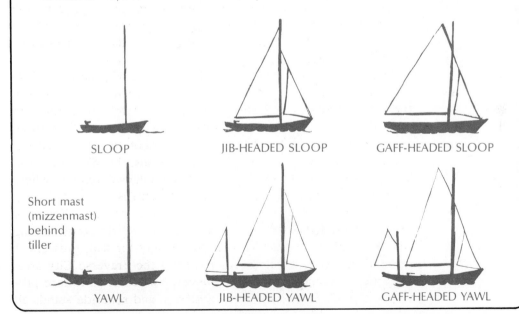

SLOOP JIB-HEADED SLOOP GAFF-HEADED SLOOP

Short mast (mizzenmast) behind tiller

YAWL JIB-HEADED YAWL GAFF-HEADED YAWL

91

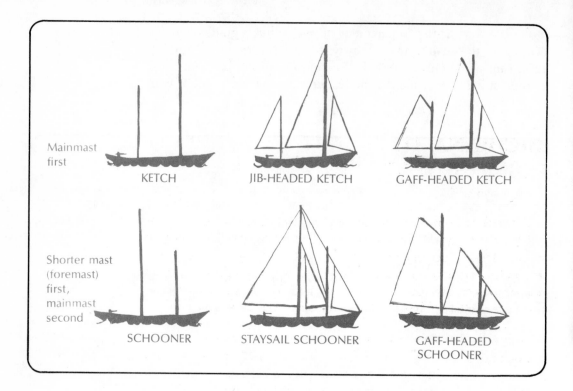

Mainmast
first

KETCH   JIB-HEADED KETCH   GAFF-HEADED KETCH

Shorter mast
(foremast)
first,
mainmast
second

SCHOONER   STAYSAIL SCHOONER   GAFF-HEADED
SCHOONER

MICHIANA TO
POINT BETSIE

THESE tiny communities mark the beginning of Michigan's claim to the longest continuous stretch of freshwater beach in the world; Berrien County in the southwest corner of the state has fifty miles of wondrous water border. However, it's largely private property until the marina at New Buffalo. Transient accommodations are available at Snug Harbor Marine, 616/469-2600.

●MICHIANA, GRAND BEACH, NEW BUFFALO

A two-mile beach backed by spectacular dunes, the kind hang-glider addicts fall for ... or from. There are 197 campsites with hot showers and the comfort works, plus a bathhouse and acres of beach parking. Two hundred acres of virgin woods have been preserved for study; the pathways between water and trees are delightful. Post Office, Sawyer, Michigan 49125. 616/426-4013.

●WARREN DUNES STATE PARK

Follow Harbert Road west from Red Arrow Highway; right on the lake.

●PICNIC SPOT

In the handsome quarters of the Cook Energy Center (Indiana and Michigan Electric Company) they put on an intriguing, vivid show. Through the use of three multimedia theaters, visitors see a few sides of the energy story they may not have encountered before— and the case for nuclear energy is not the whole story. Information on solar heat for your home, for example, is obtainable at the center.

●BRIDGMAN

Security regulations will not permit a tour of the nuclear plant itself, but you can stare point-blank at the layout through a large glass window and are given a short course on the what-where-and-whys.

Admission to the center is free and all comers are invited to use the patio for a lunch spot. Bring your own or buy snacks and soft drinks at the counter. Throughout the year, community and public service groups put on special displays; you might wind up at an art show. Open Monday to Friday 10:00–5:00, Sundays 11:00–5:00, January to May, October and November. Summertime visitors, June through September, will find it closed on Mondays and Tuesdays. Closed December and holidays.

Also at Bridgman: The U.S. Moyes, Inc. hang glider factory encourages tours. 11522 Red Arrow Highway. 616/426-3100.

LAKESIDE PARK ● Picnics but no camping at the end of Glenlord Road.

BENTON HARBOR– ● Twin cities on the lake and on the St. Joseph River, once a major
ST. JOSEPH grain-shipping port. Father Marquette stopped here, as did Robert de LaSalle, the explorer. When LaSalle's ship the *Griffin* didn't show up (the first known sailing ship lost to the lakes), he turned on his heels and headed for Canada, the first white man to cross through Michigan's dense forests.

Easy access made St. Joseph a popular resort center during the years of the late 1800s to early 1900s. A religious community calling themselves the House of David drew special attention because of their zeal, beards, and talent at baseball. The model train that once took passengers around a small park is now closed, though.

Berrien County is jammed with fruit; it's no surprise that the world's largest noncitrus fruit market is right here, 1891 Territorial Road. The St. Joseph Art Association's Museum at 600 State Street opens six days a week with shows that change monthly, and history buffs might like to see the Josephine Morton Memorial House, built in 1849 at 501 Territorial Road. Open twice a week (Thurs. 1:00–4:00, Sun. 2:00–4:00) during the summer. Admission is free but groups are asked to call in advance. 616/925-7185.

Three parks give ample chances to view the water as you munch lunch. In Lake Bluff Park on State and Lake Bluff Avenue in St. Joseph, you might be treated to a band concert if you come Sun-

day afternoon or evening. Edgewater Park in Benton Harbor and another one just up U.S. 33 are close to town.

Guides at Sarett Nature Center on the Paw Paw River flood plains will take you hiking into the tall grass along the marshes, explaining as they lead the way. Not open on Mondays. 3200 Benton Center Road, Benton Harbor, Michigan 49022. 616/927-4832.

Boats, boat, boats. There are over 600,000 boats registered in Michigan and half of them seem to come to Benton Harbor–St. Joe on the same day. St. Joseph's official Harbor of Refuge has fuel, restrooms, dock attendant, haul-out facilities, tank pump-out. 616/983-5432. Large new breakwater and marinas available to the public can take care of hundreds of sailors every day. Need a boat? Plenty of rentals, charters.

Several big events dot the summer: the Blossomtime Festival at the end of April or beginning of May; the Western Amateur Golf Championship Tournament at Pointe o' Woods Country Club (now past its 80th annual play); the Venetian Festival in July; and the Harvest Festival & Tri State Regatta that highlights Labor Day weekend (a Chicago–Michigan City, Indiana–St. Joseph meet). Write Chamber of Commerce, 685 W. Main Street, Benton Harbor, Michigan 49085. 616/925-0044.

On Lake Michigan, 3½ miles west on County Road 378. One hundred trailer and tent sites, electricity, showers, bathhouse, community buildings, and park store near the wide sandy beach. ● COVERT TOWNSHIP PARK

Located on 326 acres four miles south of South Haven on U.S. 31 with 205 campsites next to dunes and beach with all the modern conveniences. Remember, half the campsites can be reserved in advance. This being a popular spot, plans should be made *well* in advance! Call 616/637-2788, or write to Post Office, South Haven, Michigan 49090. ● VAN BUREN STATE PARK

The town's brochures are blue to remind folks that eighty percent of Michigan's blueberries are grown in Van Buren County and that South Haven is the site of the biggest, juiciest blueberry fest in the country come July. In past years South Haven has been a ● SOUTH HAVEN popular escape place for Chicagoans; a spot for grand hotels and incoming cruise ships. They came for the bright lights and social action, now the attention centers on fruit picking or fishing off the pier for coho ... or just sitting on the sand to watch the sunsets. Three town beaches are open to the public: South Beach at the foot of Michigan Avenue, Packard Park off North Shore Drive, and North Beach also off North Shore Drive and Oval.

The Liberty Hyde Bailey Museum is an 1850s house with *special* gardens—and no wonder; it was the boyhood home of famed horticulturist and educator Lib Bailey who headed Cornell University's agrischool. 903 S. Bailey Street, open Tues. and Fri. 2:00–4:30 or by appointment. Call 616/637-2991.

The Lake Michigan Maritime Museum is a renovated houseboat, a floating showcase for the historic arts and crafts of the lake, memorabilia, and things nautical. Open all summer but hours subject to change. Dyckman at the bridge, 616/637-8087.

For Blueberry Festival and Black River canoeing details, write to the Chamber of Commerce, South Haven, Michigan 49090.

There are two picnic spots between South Haven and Douglas, one at 121st Street west of 70th, the other at 126th Street. Both sites are on Lake Michigan.

DOUGLAS–SAUGATUCK • Another set of civic twins sharing a common ambience, the Douglas–Saugatuck combination has been drawing a choosey summer population since the days when it was a stop on the Chicago interurban and a port for the grand cruise ships of the lakes. Now the fair-weather crowd comes in yachts and MGs to shop in ultra-creative boutiques or dine in quietly classy restaurants. After that they go to paint pictures of the dunes and show their works in the July art shows.

Coiling through a particularly lovely notch in the high dunes, the Kalamazoo River offers canoeists and float boaters a shining path inland through placid meadows and sheltering trees. All of this land was forested at one time, supporting a score of sawmills, but fire and greed wiped out the pine crop. Farming and tourism have been mainstays ever since.

Visit the S.S. *Keewatin* and pretend you're about to set off for Cleveland. The mahogany paneling, stained glass skylights, polished brass, and deck chairs—even the linens—seem ready to go. This 350-foot Great Lake survivor was a 1907 coal burner, reduced now to taking sightseers on imaginary tours. Open daily, May-October, 10:00 AM to 4:30 PM. Box 511, Douglas, Michigan 49406. 616/857-2151, ext. 26.

At the same site the *City of Douglas* takes passengers up the river and out to the lake for breezy sightseeing. Three trips a day for a little over an hour.

Queen of Saugatuck, another tour boat, 650 Water Street, also offers three trips daily during the summer season.

For the history buff, there's Saugatuck Historical Museum, 403 Lake Street. Open Sat. 10:00–5:00, Mon.-Fri., Sun. 12:00–4:00.

Valleau Studios is a brass factory and gift shop that looks like a plantation house set in a cornfield, but here's where all those lovely antique reproductions sold in Greenfield Village are made. The family-run operation uses highly specialized sand-casting methods to make hydraulic fittings, "antique" toys, candlesticks, and more. Tours are given all year, but it would be wise to call ahead. 3534 63rd Street. 616/857-2128.

Season fun specials: Saugatuck's little mid-village park rings with two band concerts on Sundays, 3:00 and 8:00 PM. A Gilbert and Sullivan Festival is part of the theater fare at the Red Barn. Call 616/857-3601 for plays, place, and prices. The Venetian Festival naturally includes a bright parade of boats; last Saturday in July. Art shows on July Saturdays, and the Flea Market on 64th Street goes on Saturday and Sunday all summer.

The zippy ride in a dune schooner you've always craved is ready near Goshen Lake off old U.S. 31. The dune-woods trip includes a stop at the top for panoramic picture-taking. From 9:00 till dusk on weekdays, noon on Sunday. If in doubt call 616/857-2253.

Names that stand on either side of the channel opening into Lake Macatawa and to Holland—Michigan's Dutch treat. ●MACATAWA–OTTAWA BEACH

HOLLAND ● They grow millions of tulips, make and sell thousands of wooden (klompen) shoes, manufacture Delftware and cheese, and fill the phone book with names like Vanderveer. It could be the Netherlands, but it's all-American Holland, Michigan, settled by Dutch and remaining as true as possible to its heritage.

Holland was settled by refugees from the Netherlands, led by Albertus Van Raalte, who found just what they wanted in this locale: good farm land and access to a wide blue horizon. As people of the sea they were loathe to leave their boats too far behind them. The beginning years were extremely rough and many did not survive, but the Dutch are not easily defeated. Not even a disastrous fire that leveled everything but the handsome white church on the hill kept Holland from growing. The church, the historic Ninth Street Christian Reformed Church, is a place to hear Dutch-language services on special occasions.

At ninety years, the church (dubbed the "Pillar Church" because of its splendid wooden columns) is younger than the authentic 213-year-old Netherlands windmill, "De Zwaan." One of the last mills allowed to go out of the country after World War II, the handsome relic was used as a sniper post during the war and has the bullet holes to prove it. Costumed guides tell you more about its history and about the workings of the giant "wings." The twelve-stories-tall mill is reflected in the eastern shallows of Lake Macatawa, a vantage point that photographers happily make the most of. A miniature Dutch village, klompen dancers, gardens, canal bridge, and draaimolen (merry-go-round) are also part of Windmill Island Park. Corner of 7th and Lincoln Avenue. Open May through October, limited hours after Labor Day. 616/396-5433.

Holland is a neat, trim, and pious town that is *very* quiet on Sundays and puts on the state's biggest annual festival. The mid-May Tulip fest is, in fact, just slightly behind the Rose Parade in Pasadena and the Mardi Gras in New Orleans in popularity.

On each day of the four-day bulb-blitz there's a traditional street scrubbing session and hundreds of young folks in authentic Dutch costume kicking and clapping their way through country dances in squares and circles three blocks long. Parades of kids and bands and floats—and of course acres of tulips carefully guided into bloom at just the right moment. The colorful show lasts in one way or another for the whole summer.

Another place to watch klompen dancers and wander through

De Zwaan windmill

99

Dutch Village

Dutch surroundings is in the Dutch Village on the north side of town, along U.S. 31. Authentically done ¾ths scale buildings have thatched roofs or red tiles to cover shops and exhibits. A massive Amsterdam street organ plays with marvelous gusto and the ever-present miniature windmill presides over more gardens. The Village also has a good restaurant.

Just up the road is one of Michigan's largest bulb farms, Veldheers; another floral treat is Nelis Farm, close by.

There are two places to see wooden shoes made: at the De-Klomp Wooden Shoe and Delftware factory at 257 E. 32nd Street (616/396-2292), or the Wooden Shoes Factory on U.S. 31 By-Pass and 16th Street (616/396-6513).

You can learn more about going Dutch at the Netherlands Museum, an old and gentle house overflowing with treasures of Holland's heritage. Authentic old-world rooms house treasures from the Netherlands Pavillion of the New York World's Fair. Open 9:00 AM to 5:00 PM daily, Sunday at 11:30–5:00 during May-September. Small admission.

The Baker Furniture Museum on the corner of 6th Street and Columbia Avenue has a no-pretense display. Furniture that served as style models, antiques, and so forth are side-by-sideboard, arm-chair-by-end table in close array. An absolute must for students of interior decor or would-be cabinet makers. 616/392-8761.

The privately-owned Poll Museum on U.S. 31 north of the city is one man's outstanding collection of antique and classic autos, fire trucks, coaches, model trains, bottles, and grand miscellany. Open May 1 to October, Monday through Saturday.

DeGraff Nature Center, a pause the kids will enjoy, is right in town. Graafschap Road at 26th Street. 616/392-4863.

Hope College Summer Repertory Theater has offerings of a different genre; plays and musicals from early July until September. 12th and Columbia Streets. 616/392-1449.

There are also Tuesday evening concerts in Kollen Park, the Ottawa County Fair, and other highlights that the Chamber of Commerce will be glad to let you in on. 7 E. 8th Street, Holland, Michigan, 49423. 616/392-2389. (But don't expect miracles. If you want to go to the Tulip Festival, make *that* plan early!)

Access ramps on both sides of Lake Macatawa (one of them in Kollen Park) are paved and suitable for all trailerable boats.

Not many trees but towering dunes, a super beach, and 342 camp-   • HOLLAND
ground sites. There's good perch fishing if you don't get here at   STATE PARK
coho time. Very popular park; reserve far in advance.

Picnic spots are at Tunnel Park a little north of the state park on Lake Shore Avenue and up past Port Sheldon and Zwemer Beach near Fillmore Street.

Another wide and wondrous beach, this real crowd-puller has a   • GRAND HAVEN
pier for fishing on Lake Michigan plus frontage on the Grand River.   STATE PARK
Bring your beach umbrella; there's not much shade. The 170 campsites have electricity, showers, and all the rest, and are used to capacity during the summer months. Reserve early. Post Office, Grand Haven, Michigan 49417. 616/842-6020.

Ferrysburg, Grand Haven, and Spring Lake cluster at the mouth of   • GRAND HAVEN
the Grand River and only the natives really know where one community begins or the other ends. Area history is full of Indian legends and odd connections with famous names. For example, a French fur trader named Laframboise was shot by the Indians and buried in Grand Haven by his Indian wife who continued to deal in pelts. Her daughter married the commander of Fort Mackinac, thus becoming the sister-in-law of the future president Franklin Pierce. Another famous local was Dr. Vanderveen, the Grand Haven physician who attended Lincoln when he was assassinated.

As with all these coastal communities, Grand Haven had a history tied up with boating even before the tourist trend took hold. One of the saddest moments for the town came when a Coast Guard escort was sunk during World War II; all hands were from Grand Haven, and the moment is remembered with solemn ceremony every August 4.

On Dewey Hill is a watery artwork said to be the world's largest musical fountain. Electrically controlled patterns of spouting water and lights with synchronized melodies dance nightly for summer visitors, one of the best shows along the "edge."

Summer fun: "Up in Central Park" Art Festival, a run of art, craft, flower shows, and concerts from mid-July through August. The Coast Guard Festival (parades, water shows, special fountain display) is during the first week of August. For more information, write to the Chamber of Commerce, One Washington Avenue, Grand Haven, Michigan 49417. 616/842-4910.

The banks of the Grand River have a number of access sites suitable for most boats. The access at Stearns Bayou, however, is for canoes and car-toppers.

The Grand Haven Harbor of Refuge offers over thirty transient berths, gasoline, water, electricity, showers, pump-out, dock attendant. 616/846-5590.

A small park at Ferrysburg is for lake-watchers.

P. J. HOFFMASTER STATE PARK • On the Muskegon–Ottawa county line, this 1,043 acres of park with an abundance of trees has swimming, picnicking, and a nature center. For the users of the 333 campsites, flush toilets, hot showers, electricity, and sanitation station. Very popular. Post Office, Muskegon, Michigan 49441. 616/798-3711.

MUSKEGON • Ever hear of log rustling? When young Muskegon was growing into the rip-roaring center of hard lumbering competition, log rustling was as rampant in the vicinity as cattle rustling on the range.

Fur-trading woodsmen and Indians conducted the pioneer businesses of Muskegon, but lumbering made it boom. With forty-seven sawmills cutting up the woods, the matter of telling which logs belonged to which company became an issue. At first every logger put his own crude cuts into the side of the log (like a brand), but by the time it had floated downstream and bumped into hundreds of other logs, the cuts were often mutilated beyond recognition ... or changed intentionally by rustlers. Later each company cut its logo into the butt end of the log, only to have thieves haul the timbers out, saw off the ends and re-mark them.

Logs were raw money. After the Civil War, railroad expansion needed ties (31,000 miles of track in one eight-year period) and from Chicago straight across the prairie the new trains also had to bring more lumber to supply the towns they touched. As the ravenous consumption of Michigan's forests increased, Muskegon broke the world's record with 665,450,000 cut feet ... and grew extremely rich.

That was 1887, however, and no way could Mother Nature survive the exploitation. By 1890 (only *three* years later!) the trees were gone, the mills closed; unemployed loggers drifted out of town. Rows of houses stood empty and the city that once boasted of forty millionaires and more silk hats per capita than any other city in the U.S. sank into a deep depression.

One lumberman who didn't leave was Charles H. Hackley, a name you get quickly acquainted with as you visit Muskegon. Hackley, playing cheerleader to nearly deserted stands, organized a group to encourage new businesses to settle in Muskegon and donated much of his own vast fortune to making civic improvements. So successful were these efforts that today Muskegon man-

Hackley House

ufactures everything from refrigerators to bowling equipment, crane hoists, and iron.

Hackley's house at 484 West Webster is a thoroughly Victorian dream open to the nostalgic public. An elegant porte-cochere (notice that the horse was under a roof while passengers went up the uncovered steps! Details.) and stately turreted corner; glorious gingerbread and a round front window.... Those chimneys lead to seven fireplaces, each one a separate creation in tile and lavishly carved wood. Tiffany glass touches, of course. The house was selected as one of the top restoration projects in the country in 1975.

Next door, the Thomas Hume house is a tad less flamboyant, but it has a fancy adjoining stables that you might want to move into. Hume was a business partner as well as a neighbor of Hackley. Both places are open Wednesday, Saturday, and Sunday, 2:00–4:00, from "Hackley Day" (May 25) through August. Admission charged. Call 616/744-8170 or 722-7578.

All blocks between Sixth and Second streets, Webster and Clay, have been designated as part of an historic district. Along with the Hackley and Hume houses, there's an old fire house, the Hackley Art Gallery, and Hackley Library. (Are you suprised? There's also a Hackley Street, Hackley Hospital, and more. The man gave away *millions*.)

Art lovers will appreciate the gallery's sharp choices Monday-Saturday 9:00 AM to 5:00 PM; Sunday 2:00–5:00. 296 W. Webster, 616/722-6924.

Muskegon's thoughtful regard for the old and irreplaceable— even when valuable real estate is being sacrificed—is extremely commendable. The historic district and Indian cemetery, both close to midtown, are cases in point. Muskegon Mall, one of the first city-savers to incorporate buildings as they were and gather them all under one roof, is a delight.

In another preservation project, the Michigan Theater's (Frauenthal Center Building, 407 West Western Avenue) elaborate terra cotta interior decor has found new friends. The West Michigan Theater Organ Club sponsors programs on a magnificent old-timer along with silent movies and sing-a-longs. To find out about such programs and other events, write to the theater or call 616/722-2113.

At the Muskegon County Museum, Indian arrows and leather vests mix with pioneer pots and axes plus a horde of old photos. 30 Muskegon Avenue, 616/722-0278. June to September, 10:00 AM to 4:00 PM, Tuesday through Saturday. Slightly different schedule during the winter.

Captain Jonathan Walker, immortalized by Whittier as the "Man With the Branded Hand," is given further tribute in a monument near the entrance to Evergreen Cemetery, off Irwin Street. The brave abolitionist was caught helping slaves escape to Bermuda and "S.S." (slave stealer) was branded on his hand by order of the Federal Court.

A Farmer's Market opens every Tuesday, Thursday, and Saturday at 7:00 AM, and a Flea Market on Wednesdays. 700 Yuba Street, off Bus. 31 and Eastern Avenue. 616/722-3251.

Fishing for lake trout, chinook salmon (fifteen- to forty-pounders in September and October), coho, steelhead, and more, is such a Muskegon passion that nonfisherpeople stay in the closet. West Michigan's largest launching ramp, on Giddings Street near downtown, has room for 214 cars to park near a ramp that will handle anything. There are two more on the same side of Muskegon Lake off Lakeshore Drive. Look for signs as you go west.

Some transient accommodations are available at Municipal marina; haul-outs available through arrangments with dock master. Water, electricity, restrooms, showers, holding tank pump-out. 616/722-3361.

As Muskegon is now one of the state's largest industrial shipping ports, pleasure boat owners are urged to use extra vigilance.

Big summer event is the Seaway Festival, centering around the Fourth of July. Doesn't concentrate only on the sea, but includes a Polka Fest, beer tents, village market, GIANT parade, and more than a few boats.

Two-and-one-half miles of that continuously on-rolling marvel, the ● MUSKEGON STATE Lake Michigan beach, plus a long stretch on the Muskegon channel. A beauty of a park with hardwoods and pines, wood trails and
PARK

105

dunes. A restored blockhouse is supposed to give you an all-around panoramic view but doesn't quite make it because the trees are so tall. Fun to explore anyway. The bathhouse is new and sleek, the 357 (a city!) campsites have all the services. Boat dock and launching site are part of the package. 1,125 acres. Post Office, North Muskegon. 616/744-3480.

Lakeshore Drive from here to Whitehall is travel-folder scenic. Go slow; enjoy!

DUCK LAKE STATE PARK • The unimproved Duck Lake Park has some frontage on Lake Michigan plus land on both sides of the Duck Lake Channel. Very limited facilities, no camping. You can fish, swim, and picnic all you want, however.

WHITE LAKE: WHITEHALL, MONTAGUE • Two communities encasing the eastern tip of the lake: antique shops, boat ramps, and a couple of very special attractions.

One is the White River Lighthouse Museum in Montague. Nearby trees tower above the light, but the quaint old building is filled with marine and lumbering bits and pieces and worth an unhurried stop.

The other is the Blue Lake Fine Arts Camp, a top-ranking facility and the second largest of its kind in the country. Top performers (Victor Borge, Roberta Peters, Count Basie) have appeared on summer programs; concerts, chorales, recitals reflect the camp's diverse curriculum. Sit under a roof or bring your blanket to spread on the lawn. Partly supported by the Michigan Council for the Arts. Write to Blue Lake Highlights, 110 West Colby, Whitehall, Michigan 49461 or call 616/894-9026.

CLAYBANKS MEMORIAL TOWNSHIP PARK • A peaceful spot on Stoney Lake, off Stoney Lake Road, just east of the Claybanks County Scenic Drive.

LITTLE POINT SABLE LIGHTHOUSE • On the south side of Silver Lake State Park, this bright red brick structure makes for great pictures against the blue sky and lake.

SILVER LAKE STATE PARK • If you were turtle-size this would be the Sahara. A hugh beach faces Lake Michigan, with more on Silver Lake; high dunes provide wind-swept views, and there's a beautiful woods. Full facilities for

249 campsites; a store for more groceries close by. Post Office, Mears, Michigan 49436. 616/873-3083.

Sand dune rides—calm ones or "thrillers"—are available at the east end of Silver Lake at a place called Mac Woods.

A shoreline picnic site on Ridge Road just north of Harrison Road. ● CEDAR TOWNSHIP PARK

The only port between Ludington and White Lake sees only a ● PENTWATER pleasure boat trade. The small, sedate community is one of the oldest resort spots on this side of Michigan, its streets and home-sites platted originally by Charles Mears. Mears was one of those all-talented pioneers who operated lumber mills, produced bricks, planned the town, grew cranberries, ran a ferry boat, and invested in real estate. The adjacent state park bearing his name is on land donated to Michigan by his daughter. A free band concert on summer Thursday evenings in the village park is one tuneful tra-dition; the Asparagus Festival held during the second week of June in nearby Hart is a tradition of a different flavor.

For sailors, Pentwater's harbor has a dozen transient accom-modations, gasoline and diesel fuel, water, electricity, restrooms, showers, dock attendant. 616/869-8301.

Small as coastal parks go, Mears lacks woods but not beach; 179 ● CHARLES MEARS campsites on fifty acres plus all the facilities. Post Office, Pent-   STATE PARK water, Michigan 49449. 616/869-2051.

Lakeside picnic spot on Lake Shore and Deren roads. ● SUMMIT TOWNSHIP PARK

Eastern lair of an endangered species: the lake-crossing ferry. ● LUDINGTON

The best of all tourist attractions are the least contrived. They are functional, practical operations that the public can not only watch but be a part of. Locks at Sault Ste. Marie, bridges at Mack-inac, Port Huron, and Detroit, and the car-train ferry across Lake Michigan are cases in point. If you can't get on yourself, it's still fun to watch cars drive up the spiral ramp at Ludington and dis-appear into the auto deck, and then wave good-bye as the ferry leaves for Wisconsin ports.

Even better is to go along. It *could* be an ocean cruise. Sailing out of land sight for hours, you can relax in a deck chair and smile over the around-Chicago traffic you're missing. Have dinner on board or even rent a private cabin and snooze. Six-and-one-half hours later you arrive in places called Manitowoc or Kewaunee.

Motorists save over a million gallons a year this way, but the struggle to save the coal-burning ferries seems not to impress Washington; 1983 appears to be the last summer for the ferries.

Meanwhile, back on the dock, Ludington has civic charms, museums, fests, and a history that sounds like Pentwater's. One strong-willed and energetic man, James Ludington, platted the town, owned the lumber mill, and decided to put his name on the whole project. On the narrow peninsula between Lake Michigan and Pere Marquette Lake a large white cross marks where the pioneer priest died and was buried for a while (the body later transferred to St. Ignace).

Because of its halfway-up position on the east side of the lake and its ready supplies of food and fuel, Ludington enjoyed boom years as a port and is now the center of a flotilla of fishing boats. The $50,000–top prize American Salmon Derby is held here in late August and early September.

The Mason County Historical Society has done a noble job of gathering irreplaceable Mason buildings for preservation in White Pine Village. The county's first courthouse, a jail, a one-room school, the blacksmith's shop, a farmhouse, and other buildings have been taken from their earlier sites and arranged to look as though they'd always been together. The village is open from Memorial Day to Labor Day and for a few special occasions during the rest of the year. In June they hold a vintage car exhibit; July's Heritage Week includes music and entertainment; bluegrass is featured in August. Write for the details. Open 11:00 AM to 5:00 PM Monday through Saturday, 1:00 PM to 7:00 PM on Sundays. Open Holidays. 1687 South Lake Shore Drive, Ludington, Michigan 49431. 616/ 843-4808.

The present courthouse, by the way, was built in 1893 and is well worth a step inside. If you fancy old houses with lots of Victorian gingerbread, gaze at the home on Court and Lavinia Streets.

Band concerts and ice cream socials are popular summer treats

in Lakefront Park, usually on Wednesday evenings until mid-August; the Western Michigan County Fair runs during the second August week.

Township Park, Stearns City Park, Waterworks City Park, and two picnic sites on nearby Lincoln Lake are available; take your choice and unload the hamper.

Over four thousand splendid acres that would turn any hothouse ● LUDINGTON STATE flower into an outdoor type. In addition to more than three miles PARK of Lake Michigan beach, there are four miles of shore on Hamlin Lake. Hike the scenic trail to the lighthouse or fish for bass, blue-gills, walleyes, and perch. Bathhouse, playgrounds, two camp-grounds, boats for rent, and launching site. The 398 campsites are near high dunes and wide vistas. Post Office, Ludington, Michigan 49431. 616/843-8671.

On Lake Michigan, follow U.S.F.S. 5209 to 5211. For trailers or ● MANISTEE FOREST tents: campstoves, toilets, water, swimming. CAMPGROUND

With ships and markets on one side and an endless El Dorado of ● MANISTEE trees on the other, it's little wonder that the cities of the shore had early histories as lumber camps. There were over a thousand sawmills in Michigan by 1860; hundreds of them were along the Lake Michigan coast. *Manistee* means "Spirit of the Woods" and the settlement was, like the rest, a lumber town.

The fires that hit Wisconsin and Chicago in 1871 did their dam-age across Michigan, too, as we've already noted, but bad forest management—or no management at all—finished off the lumber business. In Manistee a new chemical industry, based on enormous deposits of salt, magnesium, and gypsum took its place.

More to the visitor's taste is the fruit-growing business, a West-ern Michigan success story. Thanks to the wide, temperature-toning waters of the lake, winds blowing across the northern states lose some of their chill factor while they deliver thick blan-kets of protective snow . . . and insure sumptious crops of cherries, apples, and peaches. The strawberry yield per acre is the highest east of the Rockies.

Manistee's refurbished downtown shopping blocks are bright

with Victorian charms and modern come-ons. At 425 River Street, the blue and white shop with the "Lyman Drug Company" sign is a neat branch of the Manistee County Historical Museum, whose main building is the Holly Water Works plant, 1st near Cedar Street. An outstanding collection of records, deeds, and data; exhibits relate to the lumbering era, Indian relics, and geegaws you may remember from great grandpa's house. Water Works open daily during the summer; "Drug Company" open all year. 616/723-5531.

The National Register of Historic Places lists Manistee's Ramsdell Theater, built in 1903. To see the building you must attend a play, which is easy to arrange since their (the Manistee Civic Players) long season stretches from February to November. 101 Maple Street, P.O. Box 32, Manistee, Michigan 49660. 616/723-9948.

Access to Lake Michigan and Manistee Lake is on Arthur Street, a large paved ramp managed by the city with ample parking. A second site is at East Lake.

A large number of transient accommodations is available at the Manistee Harbor of Refuge designated marina. Gasoline, water, electricity, showers, restrooms, dock attendant, pump-out. 616/723-6491.

Summer specials: National Forest Festival, first week in July. Ask about the Portage Lake Panfish Contest, the Boyer Cup Sailboat Race, and more. Chamber of Commerce, U.S. 31 and Mason Street.

ORCHARD BEACH STATE PARK • A scenic setting on a bluff overlooking Lake Michigan two miles north of Manistee, with a wide variety of hardwoods and evergreen, although the woods aren't what you'd call dense. On 201 acres, 175 breezy well-equipped campsites. Post Office, Manistee, Michigan 49660. 616/723-7422.

Lake Shore Road's pleasant drive north turns right into Cresent Beach Road, turns left and becomes Portage Drive. This is to get you around Portage Lake, taking you past Onekama Village (with lakeside park and access site). Keep circling left and you'll probably find the entry channel, lighthouse, and breakwaters to fish from.

Ends westward near Point Lookout.   COUNTY ROAD • 5099

A lumber community that didn't grow into something big ... and • ARCADIA
kept its peace. Arcadian Marshlands Water Santuary is a nearby
roost for bird lovers.

M-22 up from Manistee County is lovely, scenic driving. A *super*
lookout spot is right on the county line, more ahead. Both Lower
and Upper Herring lakes spreading near the road have gravel access ramps for smaller boats.

An over-the-back-fence neighbor of Frankfort at the south end of • ELBERTA
Betsie Lake. Elberta (same name as the peach) and Frankfort,
blessed with benevolent air currents, high take-off points, and soft
places to land, have become hang glider meccas and the site of
national meets. You can find out more in Benzonia, seven miles
east, where a local firm makes gliders, gives lessons, and knows
where the best hills are. For more information, call Eco Flight
Gliders, 616/892-5070.

The National Gliding and Soaring Festival is the last week in
June.

Water gateway to the smallest county in the state. After years as • FRANKFORT
an Indian camp and then a lumber town, Frankfort settled early
into the tourist business. It's easy to see why. Nearby Crystal Lake
has long been considered one of Michigan's inland queens and the
Sleeping Bear Dunes—incredible mountains of sand—are just
ahead.

The Ann Arbor Railway System's car ferry to Wisconsin (an
operation that will be phased out one of these years) offers half-
day voyages with deck-strolling, dining, and even state rooms for
those who want to be alone. We hope those days return.

Adjacent to the Coast Guard station, lighthouse, and breakwater,
a simple cross marks the spot where Pere Marquette may have
died. (Yes, you heard the same story in Ludington. Not even historian Bruce Catton could sort out the mystery.)

Municipal harbor facilities include a dozen transient accommodations, gasoline and diesel fuel, water, electricity, restrooms,
showers, haul-out, pump-out, dock attendant. 616/352-9051.

Summer treat: National Gliding and Soaring Festival, mentioned above.

Bike path on M-22 north.

PICNIC SPOT • On Crystal Lake, a very short drive east of M-22 on South Lakeshore Drive.

POINT BETSIE • You can go right down to the water but not right up to the light. LIGHTHOUSE A retired, lived-in facility surrounded by cyclone fencing and no-trespassing signs, but still posing for pictures like a proud beauty. Turn at Point Betsie Light Road off M-22 as you round the west end of Crystal Lake.

Point Betsie Lighthouse

SAND, SAND EVERYWHERE . . .

It is sand that makes the water's edge a human place. Waves may pound majestically against bare rocks and be fun to watch or photograph, but with the smooth padding of sand a sea or lake becomes an intimate, surrounding thing, tugging at your toes, inviting you to melt and listen to voices from another realm.

The main ingredient of our planet, this pliable, scrunchy stuff is not an element, it's a condition: rock worn down to grain-size . . . the plentiful evidence of how wind, water, heat, and ice are grinding down mountains and chewing away at "solid" stone.

In order to qualify as sand a particle must be larger than 1/16 millimeter and smaller than 2 millimeters (8/100ths of an inch). *Silt* is finer than sand; *granules* are larger.

Scoop up a handful and you are holding a whole world of rocks and minerals. Granite, feldspar, and mica are there; even gold in miniscule amounts. Quartz accounts for nearly ninety percent of Michigan sand. Tough, chemically resistant quartz gives beaches their lustrous glare and holds together after most substances have gone to dust. In other localities a different material may dominate deserts and seasides, such as the coral dunes of Bermuda, the black lava of Hawaii, or the white gypsum of New Mexico.

Winds must blow about eight miles an hour to move fine sand, and more than twenty-five miles an hour to move the coarse grains, to pitch them against an object or surface—perhaps a piece of driftwood—where they will accumulate into a dune. These minute, numberless particles may bury the item which caused the build-up (trees, forests, whole communities), but real height is elusive because sand keeps blowing off the top before vegetation has a chance to hold it down. In desert regions this relentless action, unhampered by rain, keeps a dune moving ahead, often with tragic consequences (many Africans, for example, are on the edge of the traveling Sahara). In humid Michigan, dunes are held down (stabilized) rather quickly.

The tall, tawny mounds along Lakes Michigan and Superior, plus the inland dunes south and west of Saginaw Bay, stand at the edge of a prehistoric lake which had a much higher water level. Moreover, the Sleeping Bear and Grand Sable sand piles aren't all that thick. They are called "perched" dunes since they sit on piles of rock and gravel scooped forward by an ancient glacier.

A sand dune is most certainly a fun creation, for it seems to beg for climbing, picnicking, leaping into, and challenging with a vehicle. Great for unleashed ham actors who love to pretend they are the just-shot hero toppling off the fortress wall.

Where the park management has placed boardwalks over dunes and asked visitors to stick to designated areas, it is not just to curb fun but to protect a delicate corner of our environment. With so much space open to use there is no reason to invade these essential sanctuaries.

Following the long blue edge of summer means slipping into something comfortable . . . Michigan sand. Enjoy.

You must remember, however; the dune is an extremely fragile ecological system that looks nearly empty but is not. The few scrawny plants you see, plus the insects and creatures you don't see, are struggling against mighty odds. None are unimportant.

As a hill of sand begins to take shape, tough little sprigs of beach grass start trying for anchorage. Only plants that can manage with scorching heat, gritty abrasives, and a forlorn diet can get a root-hold on a sand dune. Very extensive root systems must reach an extra distance down through the pile to locate water and also spread out to catch rain before it sinks away. When the hardy pioneer plants decay they form the mulch that allows trees and larger growth to really pin the dune down.

Most animal life on a dune is small and mousy, more likely to be seen in the cool hours of early morning or late evening. An astonishing number of insects are able to find support systems within the sands. If you can put yourself into the company of a trained naturalist (check your park programs) these tiny inhabitants will become more evident.

SLEEPING BEAR TO
WILDERNESS STATE PARK

A N unrestrained pouring out of superlatives—biggest, best, most beautiful—is hard to resist. Cliffs of sand, 440 feet above lake level at one point, interlocked with woods and glistening water; this is an exhilarating, easy-to-reach natural wonder.

Years ago one section looked more bearish than it does today and Indians explained the outline with a legend. According to their tale, forest fires in Wisconsin forced a mother bear and two cubs to swim for safety in Michigan. Mother climbed ashore and fell asleep waiting for her children, but the youngsters tired and drowned in Lake Michigan, whereupon they were transformed by the Great Spirit into the Manitou Islands.

The park's administrative offices are in Frankfort, but the Visitor's Center on M-109 north of Empire has all the information on trails, camp sites, and picnic grounds. Exhibits explaining the ecology of dunes are designed to let you know there is much more than sand involved.

The Philip Hart Nature Trail (also called the Pierce Stocking Scenic Drive) twists through a beech-maple forest, lushly carpeted with trillium and fern, to dune overlook sites that have special platforms for viewing. On a clear day you can see Point Betsie, twenty miles away.

For a real workout you'll want to climb the giant sand slope surely created just for humans who can't resist a challenge. No piece of playground equipment could ever be more fun. Soft sand grips the feet and resists all upward efforts—but hale and hearty

SLEEPING BEAR
DUNES NATIONAL
LAKESHORE

types will find the view and the satisfaction of the climb are worth it. Do not go up, however (as this sweating, panting author did), with a lot of camera equipment expecting to get a shot of Lake Michigan from the top. What you reach is a wide plateau with more sand hills ahead and more hills past those. It's a Sahara up there!

Three separate sections form the boundaries of the park. It is hoped that they will be connected in the future by scenic corridors looping around Glen Lake.

The Manitou Islands are within park boundaries; South Manitou is reached by the ferry from Leland. Although no cars are transported, there is a motorized island tour to take visitors to the tallest lighthouse on the Great Lakes, past the forlorn hulk of a grounded Liberian freighter, and through a cedar forest. Or skip the vehicle and hike along the marvelous beaches, the trails bordered with rare wildflowers. Three campgrounds for backpackers have water but no stoves. Bring a picnic lunch or dine in light informality at the Island Marina. At the Platte River and D. H. Day campgrounds there are facilities and beach access. All camping is limited to fourteen days, with a permit only; filled to capacity during the summer.

For more information write: Sleeping Bear National Lakeshore, 400 Main Street, Frankfort, Michigan 49635, or Visitors Center, Empire, Michigan 49630.

EMPIRE, GLEN • Three villages caught in the folds of Sleeping Bear's irregular lim-
HAVEN, GLEN ARBOR its. Empire took its name from a schooner that once came to its shores and stayed through the winter. The waterfront park of this tidy colony was a parting gift from the old Empire Lumber Company.

Empire is also the western end of Shore to Shore Hiking-Riding Trail, a path ambling across the northern half of the lower peninsula. Between Tawas and Empire the trail crosses lovely scenic country along the Broadman and Au Sable Rivers, through pines and hardwoods. Twelve camps, 200 miles of main path, more camps and mileage on three different spur trails. Information can be obtained from State Forest Field Offices (Tawas, Michigan 48730 or Mio, Michigan 48647) or the Department of Natural Resources (Betsie State Forest, 616/325-4611 or Au Sable State Forest, 517/348-6371). A booklet containing detailed trail maps is available from Michigan Trail Riders Association, 2864 Beitner Road, Traverse City, Michigan 49684. Cost of $5.00 includes membership in the club.

Tiny Glen Haven is a place to inquire about dune rides; it has beach access and a Coast Guard station.

Glen Arbor supplied wood to lake steamboats and cranberries to state cooks, and now sells groceries to vacationers and acts as activity center to the folks around Glen Lake. If you turn right off

At Sleeping Bear Dunes

M-22 on Westman, then left onto the county road, you come to Miller Hill Road and soon to a scenic overlook that is worth the detour. Two access sites and one campground on *beautiful* Glen Lake.

Star gazers should write to the Leelanau Observatory, part of the Leelanau School, for information on summer programs: Glen Arbor, Michigan 49636. (The road up Observatory Hill is shortly inside the gate of The Homestead, a large and posh rent-or-buy resort.)

LELAND • Cool, calm, and quietly collected little Leland is as prim as a maiden aunt can be among the noises of a new generation. Wealthy families came from Detroit and Chicago long ago, establishing an air of gentility that is still evident. Between Lake Michigan and the long, oddly-shaped Lake Leelanau, Leland is the place to catch the ferry to South Manitou Island. Two township parks face the inland lake, another set of swings and benches looks out over Lake Michigan.

A short stretch of river connects the two lakes and flows over a dam on its way out, giving a local entrepreneur an excuse to build a foot bridge and "waterfall" restaurant. People watch the gushing water and jumping coho, but they also use the bridge to photograph "Fishtown," a double row of shanties dating back to the 1800s. Just as in New England, nets dry on dockside reels; the deep-lake fishing boats are sturdy, aging veterans. There may be more souvenirs than fish sold from the gray sheds these days, but Fishtown has made its way into the National Historic Registry.

Try to land in jail before you leave town. The old and rather cute county clink has been appropriated by the Leelanau County Historical Society as a museum; it's on Chandler and River streets. Open from June 30 until Labor Day, Monday through Saturday, 10:00 AM to 3:00 PM. Write to Leland, Michigan 49654, for more information.

Leland harbor's marina has an unusually large number of berths for transient boaters. Gasoline and diesel fuel, water, electricity, restrooms, showers, pump-out, dock attendant. 616/256-9132. VHF-FM radio.

On the west side of the Leelanau peninsula, follow M-22 to North- ● PETERSON
port, then up M-201 to Peterson Park Road. TOWNSHIP PARK

Top of the "little finger" of Michigan's geographic mitten, the park ● LEELANAU STATE
has 1,044 acres, plenty of beach and space; no electricity for the PARK
forty-two rustic campsites. Post Office Box 49, Northport, Michigan 49670. 616/386-5422.

Take M-201 north from Northport, follow the signs to the light- ● LIGHTHOUSE POINT
house. This boarded up white relic was once a vital light to ships TOWNSHIP PARK
rounding into Grand Traverse Bay. No beach here; only a border
of broken stones and very few picnic tables. Still, it's delightful.

A charming village in the full sense of that overworked term. ● NORTHPORT
Great place to fill up on fruit, browse for antiques and crafts.
    In Northport's marina are three dozen transient accommoda-
tions, fuel, water, showers, electricity, dock attendant, pump-out.
616/386-5411. VHF-FM radio.

The site of an historic Indian council and early mission. ● PESHAWBESTOWN

Not very large but clearly big on civic pride, spic-and-span Suttons ● SUTTONS BAY
Bay is inviting enough to park and walk around in two bayside
parks operated by the village. And there's a dock with paved
launching ramp, room for eight transients, gasoline, pay telephone,
water, and electricity.

At Suttons Point, end of Suttons Point Road. ● COUNTY ROADSIDE PARK

At Lee Point, south of Suttons Bay, M-22 to Lee Point Road. ● HENDRYX COUNTY
    Fishing access site at M-22 and foot of Hill Top Road. ROADSIDE PARK

Next to M-22, overlooking Traverse Bay, about five miles north of ● COUNTY ROADSIDE
Traverse City. PARK

Large paved access to Traverse Bay. Another one on south end of ● ELMWOOD
Cedar Lake, for smaller boats only, both on the edge of Traverse TOWNSHIP PARK
City.

"Life is just a bowl of cherries" amounts to *much* more than a ● TRAVERSE CITY
Pollyanna phrase in northern lower Michigan's largest urban col-

ony. To Traverse City, center of a 125 million pound per year cherry crop, bowls of cherries are full of bread and butter; they pay the rent, bring home the bacon, and are reasons to celebrate. What started as an experiment in an orchard only one acre large has become big agribusiness supplying one third of the world's stock of the tasty little red gems.

In 1847 William Broadman, an early comer to these lush shores, purchased property where the city now stands and went into logging. Four years later a Chicago firm, Hannah, Lay and Company, bought Broadman out, then proceeded to pile up a fortune. Both names are on Traverse City street signs. The city's growth followed the pattern of wealth from lumbering, discovery as a delightful area to spend pollen-free summers, decline of timber, and growth of fisheries, fruit farms, and fashionable resorts.

Today commercial fisheries are nearly gone, but sportsmen, sailors, swimmers, and scuba divers take to the clear blue waters of Grand Traverse Bay. The surrounding hills and wooded trails get a permanent hold on hikers and bikers; golf addicts and tennis fans find courts and courses down every road. If you stick close to the wining-dining-shopping routine you're in the right territory. There are several classy restaurants (and any fast food outfit you could name) along with off-beat boutiques and on-beat stores. (Antiques are big.) The motel list is at least 2,000 rooms long. In short, this is one of Michigan's most popular vacation and convention meccas.

Any recreation should include a walk around Traverse City's officially-designated historic district for a long gaze at some grand vintage houses. You can't go into the Hannah Perry House at 301 Sixth Street, built in 1891, but its three-story Queen Anne styling is there to admire. The Grand Traverse County Courthouse on the southwest corner of Boardman and Washington was built in 1882 and filled the Victorian need for the elaborate, curlicued best.

A hopeful restoration project is underway at 108–112 East Front Street where the City Opera House wears a disguise of store fronts. Nothing is playing these days but visitors are invited to tour the fine old theater–dance hall where playbill advertisements still adorn the original stage curtain. Open July and August, 10:00–

12:00 AM Monday and Friday; 1:00–3:00 PM Tuesday and Thursday. Hours may vary slightly during early July. Or write Traverse City Opera, above address, Traverse City, Michigan 49684.

More historic buildings are out on the thin little peninsula running like a long green wall between the two arms of Grand Traverse Bay. The lighthouse at Mission Point is one of the oldest on the Great Lakes. No chance to go up, but do take its picture and then picnic or sunbathe on the excellent beach. In May when every cherry tree is in full bloom, the orchard-loaded peninsula is like a float in a big parade; every inch seems to be covered with blossoms.

Shades of Pavlova, one of the most unusual attractions of the Traverse City area is a 400-bird flock of elegant Mute Swans, seen in great groups during the winter and spring. Although the swans pair off in the summer, they remain close to the vicinity, practicing their own kind of ballet. Approach with extreme caution; spoiled rotten by human praise, perhaps, swans can be ugly tempered and inflict serious wounds.

Traverse City's Clinch Park includes a zoo and more swans plus an aquarium where every furred, feathered, or finned creature is a Michigan native. A small history museum, pier, and marina are part of the Clinch complex.

Next to the Park Place Motor Inn, the Cherry County Playhouse packs in summer theater-goers with names like William Shatner, Van Johnson, and Vicki Lawrence appearing on their stage. For tickets and information, write P.O. Box 661, Traverse City, Michigan 49684. 616/947-9560. Special plays for children on Friday mornings.

Or try the fare at the Old Town Playhouse, Cass at 8th, where the Traverse City Civic Players emote entertainingly. 616/947-2210.

The woods are alive with the sound of music at Interlochen National Music Camp at the Interlochen Center for the Arts. A regular schedule of art shows, dance and music recitals, concerts by well-known artists and kids whose talents are astounding. From Pete Fountain to Van Cliburn, the summer programs are worth catching. Only fifteen miles southwest of Traverse, Interlochen is a place to go if all you do is walk around among the flowers, stately pines, or the Hastings Museum. A refreshing eye and ear opener. Limited lodging available on campus: write Center for the Arts, Special Events Office, Interlochen, Michigan 49643. 616/ 276-9221.

Interlochen State Park with 550 campsites, full facilities and plenty of lake, is right across the road from the Center. Post Office, Interlochen. 616/276-9221 ext. 240.

The Traverse City harbor facilities offer transient accommodations, diesel fuel, and gasoline, all other needs except haul-out. 616/947-4471. VHF-FM radio. Boat launching ramp for all craft. Two ramps on Mission Peninsula: East Shore Road and Bowers Harbor.

THE big summer event is the National Cherry Festival, an all-out extravaganza in early July. Queens, parades, and super succulent stacks of cherry pies.

The Traverse Bay Outdoor Art Fair on the campus of Northwestern Michigan College is in late July; Northwestern Michigan Fair comes in August.

More information can be obtained from the Traverse City Area Chamber of Commerce, Traverse City, Michigan 49684. 616/ 947-5075. Ask for their rainy day folder and check out the Long Lake Paleontology Museum, the Indian Drum Museum (Boy Scouts), fish hatcheries, and scenic drives.

STATE ROADSIDE PARK ● At junction of U.S. 31 and Bunker Hill Road.

TRAVERSE CITY ● Directions say that the park is two miles east of town, but as far
STATE PARK as the stranger's eye can see it's *in* town. Thirty-nine acres, 330 campsites on U.S. 31. Tree-covered, pleasant ... and runs at capacity all summer. Post Office, Traverse City, Michigan 49684. 616/947-7193.

ACME TOWNSHIP PARK ● U.S. 31 north, past Yuba Road.

PETOBAGO STATE ● The marshy parts are state land; everything dry is private property.
GAME AREA No boat launch.

ELK RAPIDS ● In the southwest corner of Antrim County, this town is frequently referred to as "America's bit o'Ireland" because of its lakes and lush green hills. There was lumbering and an iron smelter at Elk Rapids, the first in America to ship out high-grade pig iron. In time the timber ran out and the smelter cooled; today tidy Elk Rapids warms up to travelers and smelt means only fish.

The Elk Rapids access to Lake Michigan has a paved ramp. In the marina there's room for about twelve transients, with gasoline and diesel, utilities, pump-out, showers, dock attendant. 616/264-9920.

A few campsites on the north side of town. ● VACATION VILLAGE PARK

Near the end (or the beginning) of Michigan's Polar-Equator Trail, ● KEWADIN which crosses the state as much as possible along the 45th parallel. The actual trail starts at the stone monument located on the east side of Cairn Road looking over East Arm of Traverse Bay and Elk Lake, one mile north of town. Write for hiking guide c/o M.S.U. Museum, East Lansing, Michigan 48823.

A few more campsites west of Eastport on Traverse Bay and near ● BARNES PARK the tip of beautiful Torch Lake.

At Eastport; paved ramp, large parking space. For picnics, a town- ● TORCH LAKE ship park sits about seven miles south on E. Torch Lake Drive. ACCESS

U.S. 31 north to Rex Beach Road (just past Atwood Christian ● BANKS TOWNSHIP Reformed Church), west then north on Old Dixie. Right on the PARK Bay.

Four miles south of Charlevoix: no picnicking, electricity, or flush ● FISHERMAN'S toilets, but great hiking and swimming. No motor vehicle permit ISLAND STATE PARK required for entrance.

Trailer and tent sites for forty-one camping units: campstoves, ● BELL'S BAY FOREST toilets, water, swimming, and that long blue edge. Two-and-a-half CAMPGROUND miles to Charlevoix on Lake Shore Road.

Only the gullible believe everything a Chamber of Commerce may ● CHARLEVOIX say about its town, but in the case of Charlevoix … believe it. They call it "The Beautiful"—and who can argue? Under canopies of tall trees and reflected in its crystal lake, the sparkling homes and shops of Charlevoix make it one of the prettiest spots on the map.

The community had a shaky start with its earliest arrivals, Irish fishermen who battled the Mormon settlers of Beaver Island. That dispute settled eventually and Charlevoix found its true calling as an elite retreat. The railroad to Petoskey helped considerably. It brought wealthy families from Chicago and Grand Rapids, who built twenty-room cottages and spent the season under parasols on wide lawns or yachting to Mackinac Island.

There's a tendency to drop names here. President Grant sipped lemonade on a local veranda (he is said to have asked for something stronger). Poet Sara Teasdale came; Ernest Hemingway's father brought his family to spend their summers nearby.

All those sleek boats and sunsets through the pines have had their effect on the canvas-and-brush set; a thriving art colony puts on art shows and sales that are ten cuts above average. Nor are they fixed in the common media. A shop on U.S. 31 south specializes in frames, end tables, and lamp bases made from the salvage of Lake Michigan shipwrecks.

The Beaver Island Boat Company takes passengers on a 2¼-hour trip to St. James, the island port. (See **Beaver Island** below.)

At Depot and Ferry streets is a fine little park with swimming, swings, and a pier to hang your pole from.

For the in-coming boating public looking for a refuge, the public marina is at East Jordan, down at the southern tip of Lake Charlevoix's riverlike east arm. Half-a-dozen transient accommodations and no services as of this writing.

Charlevoix summer specials: Venetian Festival (street dances, Midway), fourth weekend in July; Waterfront Art Fair, second Saturday in August.

For more information write to Chamber of Commerce, 408 Bridge Street, Charlevoix, Michigan 49720. 616/547-2101.

BEAVER ISLAND • A weather-beaten sign written in Gaelic says "one hundred thousand welcomes"; the Beaver Island Boat Company's brochures read "Come with us to America's Emerald Isle"; and the map shows a name straight from across the ocean: Donegal Bay.

Take notice. Beaver's main road is King's Highway, the town is St. James on Paradise Bay, and you visit Font (as in baptismal font) Lake or fish in the Jordan River.

The auld sod references and the biblical names are nearly all that's left of an old and often vicious struggle between early Irish settlers and the Mormon followers of one James Jesse Strang.

In 1847 Strang and a group of followers came to Beaver Island to escape from the persecution they found in other areas. They seemed to have jumped from the frying pan into fire. Irish settlers already on the island were just as hostile—if not more so—than the rest of the world. After an initial winter with little food and no real shelter (the Irish refused to give any assistance), however, the band dug in, expanded their holdings and declared Strang "King" of the whole place. There are tales that Strang took his royal status with un-humble zeal.

The colony grew to be an industrious, thriving clan of 2,500, but Strang's harsh disciplines, his five wives, and Irish ire over the fishing competition made troubles grow, too. The leader was assassinated by two of his ex-followers who spent five minutes in jail before being released as heroes. Remaining Mormons were forced to leave, having risen and fallen as a power (and the United State's only "kingdom") in a mere ten years.

Kinder words are being said about Strang these days, thanks to Beaver Island historian Doyle Fitzpatrick, Irish-sounding author of "The King Strang Story." Was he really all that bad or just a beleaguered zealot? Visitors may find clues in the Mormon Print Shop, the only building left from those dark days, and now a museum full of Island memorabilia.

You could browse quite a while through the general stores, shops that sell "shipwreck" furniture (not storm-tossed and half-broken, but made from wood found by divers), the fish sheds, and King Strang Hotel ... lunching at one of the three restaurants or listening to old-timers around the marina.

Or you can rent a bike, join an auto tour, put on your walking feet and see Lookout Point, Dr. Protar's hand-hewn house, or follow the beach trail.

The island has motels, tourist cabins, and campgrounds, plus seven inland lakes with plenty of game and panfish. Boat access sites can be found on Lake Geneserath and Fox Lake.

On the southern tip of land an 1851 lighthouse is now being used by the Charlevoix School District. At the right time of day you may be able to go up into it.

Twenty-five State Forest Campground sites are available on the east side of Beaver Island, about eight miles south of St. James. Tent and trailer sites, stoves, water, swimming, and boat launch.

The ferry from Charlevoix leaves twice daily, 8:30 AM and 12:30 PM, three times a day on July and early August Saturdays. Boats pull out of St. James at 8:30 AM and 3:00 PM. Round trips (subject to change) are $11.00 per adult, $6.00 for children (two to eleven). To take your car requires a $20.00 deposit. For more information contact Beaver Island Boat Company, 102 Bridge Street, Charlevoix, Michigan 49720. 616/547-2311. Or try Charlevoix Chamber of Commerce, 616/547-2101.

STATE ROADSIDE PARK • Faces the wide opening of Little Traverse Bay off U.S. 31.

PETOSKEY • The city was named after an Indian chief, Pet-O-Sega, supposedly meaning "rising sun." This is a little ironic because the grand beauties of the *setting* sun as it flings gold across sky and water has long been a part of local promotion.

What started as a cluster of Indian villages became a fueling station for early lake steamers, the site of a Methodist Bible camp, a health spa, and an all-round vacation center ... plus a modern city of considerable vigor. Well, modern enough to know the value of keeping one foot firmly in the past. For lovers of old houses and the whimsies of Victorian architecture, walking the streets of Petoskey's Gaslight District and adjacent Bay View is positively delicious.

The first is an ultra-smart shopping section where Lake Street and Howard plus one or two others elbow the railroad track. Spiffy bright stores and sparkling colors show off the 1800s building facades to their best. Lily Pulitizers, Pendletons, handicrafts, fudge; not an inch of chintz.

From the Gaslight District you walk uphill into Bay View, a woodsy set of streets and a park that started off as a religious revival camp where Helen Keller and other notables came to give inspiration. The summer homes these people built are beautifully preserved; gingerbread trimming is painted and quite alive in Bay View.

The Little Traverse Bay Regional Historical Society Museum in Waterfront Park is one you'll have no difficulty finding. It was built in 1892 as a depot and retains the look. Exhibits on Civil War historian Bruce Catton, Ernest Hemingway, and quill baskets made by the local Indians are part of the show. A much stared-at item is the passenger pigeon, once the most plentiful bird in North America and now so extinct that even stuffed ones are hard to find. Petoskey shipped barrels of these birds (considered a delicacy) down the lake to the gourmet restaurants of Chicago at one time. It was a lucrative business that seemed endless. However, the wanton slaughter and the loss of natural habitat with reckless lumbering practices wiped out a specie that once flocked in droves forty miles long. Museum hours during July and August, 1:00–5:00. Closed on the Fourth of July. 616/347-4235.

Out under the waters of the shining bay is a sight few visitors will ever see. A life-size crucifix has been erected in these freshwater depths, a memorial to those who died in Great Lakes shipwrecks.

Magnus Municipal Park, the next-door waterfront location, offers seventy-four campsites with campstoves, flush toilets, showers, playground, beach, and a place to park your boat trailer.

Petoskey's marina will take in many transients, has gasoline, water, electricity, showers, pump-out, and dock attendant. 616/347-6691. VHF-FM radio.

The summer gala is the Emmet County Fair, last week in August.

Write to the Petoskey Chamber of Commerce, 401 E. Mitchell, Petoskey, Michigan 49770 about additional events, or call 616/347-4150.

Continuing on M-131, the park is another place to swim and camp while you look for Petoskey stones. Ninety campsites with trimmings on 305 acres. Post Office, Petoskey, Michigan 49770. 616/347-2311.

● PETOSKEY STATE PARK

Menonaqua Beach and Romona Park are on Beach Road (you'll rejoin M-131 as you drive on); more swimming and sunning.

HARBOR SPRINGS • Trim, prim, and pretty as a Christmas card, Harbor Springs has everything for visitors to love even though catering to tourists is not what the town is all about. Between the bay-within-a-bay and a background of green bluffs are no budget buffets or big chain motels. Nineteen Harbor Springs buildings are listed in the Michigan historic preservation inventory, two in the Federal registry; the ambience is turn-of-the-century, with smart shops, art galleries, and a marina filled with *very* fine yachts. That's no surprise. An impressive list of people with names like Ford (of Wyandotte Chemicals), Reynolds (aluminum), and Gamble (of Proctor and ...) have or have had summer homes here, setting a sumptuous standard.

The Shay complex at the corner of Main and Judd streets is one of the oldies: the buildings where Ephriam Shay lived, designed, and ran his logging locomotive. Dena's Beauty Salon's quarters, built in 1890 on Gardner and Main Street, still has the ornate scroll brackets under the cornices. Another Main Street structure on the list is the Erwin Building, the first brick commercial edifice.

Chief Blackbird Ottawa Indian Museum (circa 1860), 368 E. Main, reflects the work of an extraordinarily versatile man who acted as postmaster and blacksmith while compiling books on the Indian language and legends. Open every day but Sunday, 10:00 AM to 4:00 PM. Harbor Springs, Michigan 49740. 616/526-2104.

Under the Harbor of Refuge program Harbor Springs has marina space for transients, with gasoline and diesel fuel, water, electricity, showers, haul-out, pump-out, dock attendant. 616/526-5355.

M-119 SCENIC DRIVE • If a beauty contest of the state's favorite roads were held, this tunnel through the trees with picture-window openings to the blue, blue lake would bring in an avalanche of votes.

CROSS VILLAGE • The name came from a large cross that was placed on the bluff by one of the French Jesuit missionaries in this long-time Catholic mission area. The local history is told at Great Lakes Indian Museum and library (ask about the priest who ran the 2,000-acre

church farm and slept beside his coffin) where information about Indian powwows, cemeteries, and crafts is also available. Open from mid-June to Labor Day, 9:00 AM to 6:00 PM.

That strange-looking building across the street is a legend of its own, even to being listed on the Michigan historic inventory. "Legs Inn" has a row of inverted stove legs across the front of the roof and things inside are just as eccentric, esoteric, and wild. The tavern/restaurant is built out of Lake Michigan stones and interior fixtures are turned out from tree stumps and twisted limbs without much sawing or trimming. A one-man project, full of fun and imagination.

●WILDERNESS STATE PARK

The second largest (Hartwick Pines comes first) state park in the lower peninsula is well named: there's a lot of territory here that only the most determined souls can reach. Its 7,514 acres are of wonderfully varied terrain along with an archipelago of islands marking the last turn of Lake Michigan toward the straits. The 210 campsites plus four overnight cabins with toilets and fireplaces must be reserved far, far in advance. Through masses of wild flowers, past the beaver dams, and over the ridges, hiking trails lead to refreshing remoteness, while showers, electricity, and home comforts are ready back at the campgrounds. Outdoor center, library, trailer sanitation disposal. Post Office, Carp Lake, Michigan 49718. 616/436-5381.

LAST VOYAGES

In his dramatic, absorbing book *Great Lakes Shipwrecks and Survivals*, William Ratigan points out that neither the Americans who dwell along the seaboards nor those who hail from inland plains and mountains can understand the vastness of the Great Lakes or their lethal potential. Frail sailing ships have been caught in storms by the dozens, dashed against splintering rocks and pushed under by burdens of ice, meeting catastrophe in fog and wind. Even modern vessels with sonar, radio, radar, high beam lights, and electronic whistles have had traps of water snap shut over them with terrifying swiftness.

Some random notes on the lost fleet:

THE GRIFFIN Explorer Robert Cavelier de LaSalle ordered the building of the first commercial ship on the lakes, an armed sloop, sixty feet long, with two square sails, raised quarterdeck, and five cannons. The *Griffin* was still a new ship when it left Green Bay, Wisconsin, loaded with furs, and was never seen again.

WINDJAMMERS by the hundreds set sail across the lakes until steamers put them out of business, and by the hundreds they sank or floundered on coastal rocks. Too many captains dared the storms of late November or December, pitting hopes of more profit against the dangers of killer winds. Their struggles are the framework of legend. In 1845, for example, the *Independence* was fighting through a fierce gale and icy waves on Lake Superior around Keweenaw Point while frantic passengers stamped out fires set by a cabin stove . . . knowing that the reeling ship's cargo was fifty kegs of blasting powder for the copper mines. Powder and passengers made it to port, but the *Independence* was beaten by the lake less than a decade later.

THE LADY ELGIN, a popular excursion boat carrying 300 passengers and crew members, collided with a timber-loaded schooner, the *Augusta*, about ten miles off the Winnetka, Illinois shore. Two hundred ninety-seven persons were lost in a wrenching spectacle of doomed humanity clinging to debris in heavy seas, within sight but beyond the reach of shore. It was the second worst disaster in lake history. The captain of the *Augusta*, blamed for the calamity, died when another schooner under his command, the *Mahor*, sank a few years later.

THE EASTLAND, another excursion steamer, brought the greatest tragedy of all. On July 24, 1915, in the Chicago Harbor, something drew the attention of too many passengers all at once; to the horror of

"... those grand fresh-water seas of ours, — Erie, and Ontario, and Huron, and Superior, and Michigan, — possess an ocean-like expansiveness. ..."

everyone, the boat slowly but steadily turned completely over, pinning hundreds under her hull in the Chicago River. Eight hundred thirty-five lives were lost.

FIRE, from the earliest days until the loss of the *Noronic* in Toronto in 1949 with 119 lives, has been responsible for half of the lake's twelve worst disasters.

COLLISIONS involving the *Atlantic* in 1852 (200 lives) and the *Pewabic* in 1865 (125 lives) have been heavy contributors to the death toll. Thirty years later the *Pewabic* wreck was found; its copper cargo, some dishes, etc., recovered.

THE WORST STORM is remembered in an historical marker on M-25 at Port Sanilac: "GREAT STORM OF 1913. Sudden tragedy struck the Great Lakes when a storm, whose equal veteran sailors could not recall, left in its wake death and destruction. The grim toll was 235 seamen drowned, ten ships sunk, and more than twenty others driven ashore. Here on Lake Huron all 178 crewmen on eight ships claimed by its waters were lost. For sixteen terrible hours gales of cyclonic fury made man and his machines helpless."

THE MILWAUKEE, a car ferry, disappeared in a storm in the middle of Lake Michigan in 1929 and took between forty-six to fifty-two lives.

THE BRADLEY, a 640-foot limestone carrier, was on a final trip in November 1958, heading north on Lake Michigan to her home port of Rogers City. A storm that had been brewing for several days reached full gale force when the *Bradley* neared the vicinity of Beaver Island. At 5:30 on the 18th, calls of "Mayday" came over the air to stunned radio operators; the ship was breaking in two and went down minutes later in 350 feet of water. In spite of valliant efforts against mountainous waves, thirty-three lives were lost; two survived. Most of those on board were from Rogers City.

THE EDMUND FITZGERALD gained fame far beyond Michigan when singer Gordon Lightfoot wrote a ballad about the loss of the great long ship off Whitefish Point in Lake Superior on November 10, 1975. There was a power shortage on land, the Soo locks were closed, and the *Fitzgerald*—729 feet long and loaded with iron ore pellets—was receiving instructions. "How is the other matter?" they were asked. "We are holding our own" was the answer, the last words heard from the doomed freighter. There were no survivors.

"...They are swept by Borean and dismasting blasts as direful as any that lash the salted wave; they know what shipwrecks are, for out of sight of land, however inland, they have drowned many a midnight ship with all its shrieking crew."

Ishmael in *Moby Dick* by Herman Melville

The need for skilled personnel and equipment to aid in rescue work brought about the establishment of the Life Saving Service—at first separate from but later operated by the Coast Guard. The station at Point Aux Barques, Lake Huron, was the first of five to open in 1876. Fourteen opened the following year. The number of men to compose a crew was determined by the number of oars needed to pull the largest boat used at the station.

TREASURE? Guesses are that approximately $800,000,000 worth of lost cargo, ship hulls, parts, etc. are at the bottom of the lakes. Salvage law on the lakes is not the same as on the salt seas where "finders keepers" is frequently the case. The owners of lake ships have all rights to whatever remains on the bottom unless and until they relinquish all rights in writing to the U.S. Corps of Engineers . . . who may then pass on salvage rights to someone else.

The beguiling hunt for valuables is another set of stories; tales of high risk, desperate gambles, and lives sacrificed. What the Great Lakes have taken, they have not willingly returned.

Edmund Fitzgerald
lifeboat

WESTWARD
TO MENOMINEE

A simple, beautifully designed nondenominational tribute to the heroic pioneer priest. Beams suggesting a roof—yet open to the sky—arch upward from a circular stone wall. The memory of his struggles to travel by foot and canoe into a cold, hostile territory contrast sharply with the scene the memorial faces; luxury cars and vans coming over a miracle bridge into a friendly, open land.

● FATHER MARQUETTE MEMORIAL

Very small settlement at the foot of U.S. 2 bluff. No park.

● GROS CAP

Six miles west of St. Ignace, a four-acre park site with a good view of the Mackinac Bridge.

● ROADSIDE PARK

The Forest Service maintains two campgrounds about two miles apart. One is on Lake Michigan, the other off U.S.F.S. Road 3108, almost directly north, at the west end of Brevoort Lake. Trailer, tents sites, stoves, tables. The inland location has a gravel boat ramp, suitable for smaller craft only.

● BREVOORT LAKE

Over the tree-filled gorge of Cut River, U.S. 2 skims along a steel cantilevered arch, one of Michigan's major highway bridges. Well worth a stop to explore, especially if you feel like a little exercise. The bridge, 147 feet above the river and 641 feet long, is best appreciated by climbing down the stairs on the east end and looking up. Part two of the fun is to keep on going down till you reach the soft, sandy beach.

● CUT RIVER BRIDGE

Picnic areas are on both sides of the bridge at road level and there's a foot trail for good hiking.

Cut River bridge

134

Minitown with a tiny harbor, a township park, and a few campsites • EPOUFETTE
with a walking path to Point Epoufette.

U.S. 2 west, particularly from the bridge to Naubinway, swoops
through forested domains to outline long glorious arcs of shore.
Plan to pause, park your car, and wade in the refreshing surf or
go for an hour's walk between the pines and dunes and the shining
sea.
    No benches, no facilities. Beaches beautiful in their emptiness,
unbacked by cottages or commerce, are hard to come by. Don't
hurry; it's what re-creation is all about.

Mackinac State Forest campsites on the lake for tents and trailers. • HOG ISLAND POINT
No electricity. Swimming, boat launch, stoves, and scenery. Seven
miles east of Naubinway.

Tables and grills next to the lake. • ROADSIDE PARK

Powwow site and minor fur-trading post, the name is Indian for • NAUBINWAY
"Land of Echoes." Early settlers brought echoes of their own. Established in 1800, it once was a raucous little berg with half-a-
dozen saloons, a theater, roller-skating rink, and community jail.
Fire, the ruinous plague that levels so many towns, hit Naubinway
twice, ending its days as a lumber source. Fishing, hunting, and
recreation are the big attractions now.
    Department of Natural Resources Field Office, paved boat
launching site, and more than twelve slips for transient sailors are
available. Gasoline, water, showers, electricity, pump-out, dock attendant. Pay station telephone.

About seven miles west of Naubinway, then seven miles south on • BIG KNOB FOREST
winding Big Knob Road. Tent and trailer sites, swimming, CAMPGROUND
campstoves.

No camping but a nice quiet place to munch lunch 9½ miles • GOULD CITY
south of U.S. 2 on South Gould City Road. TOWNSHIP PARK

One mile west of Gould City, a retreat in the trees. • ROADSIDE PARK

One of the Upper Peninsula's most popular fishing and resort areas, • MANISTIQUE LAKES

135

AREA ● north on Manistique Lakes Road. Big Walleye Jamboree in September, just when the fall color is at its peak.

SENEY NATIONAL ● North on M-77 (turn at the Blaney Park corner), two miles past
WILDLIFE REFUGE Germfast, this huge and varied landscape is almost exclusively for birds and beasts. No camping or boating, but there are two picnic areas, an observation tower, and a Visitor's Center ready to tell you the natural facts.

From June 15 until Labor Day an auto tour starts out at 6:00 PM. Led by a park guide, the two-hour evening meander through woods and wetlands pauses where deer, bear, waterfowl, or even bats are most likely to be seen. This cannot be taken on your own, but another tour, a short self-guided hiking trail, is marked with arrows and explanations.

The Driggs, Walsh, and Creighton trout streams are open (check the posted state laws before you cast your line) and usually there's fishing in the Show Pools from Memorial Day till September. That can change. If too many geese couples seem indifferent to nesting, then humans are ordered to back off.

ROADSIDE PARK ● Near Little Bear Creek on southbound stretch of U.S. 2.

GULLIVER ● The use of high-grade limestone—cement, glass, pharmaceuticals, soap, paint—is nearly unlimited, and Gulliver's rich limestone quarries operated by the Inland Steel Company produce over 350 million tons of stone a year, loading up scores of great freighters at their Port Inland facilities. Two little parks are located on the opposite shores of Gulliver Lake, one near U.S. 2 and the other off Lakeshore Road.

At Seul Shoix Point a sturdy white old lighthouse likes to have its picture taken. Pronounced SISHwah, the term means "only choice." Not many picnic facilities here, but you are welcome to break out the sandwiches.

DUTCH JOHN'S ● Another township park on the shore. Detour slightly off U.S. 2
POINT onto Marblehead Pit Road, turn south at park sign.

MANISTIQUE ● U.S. 2 does not run swiftly through Manistique but seems to wind around town as if trying to show you the place. Over a puzzling

"siphon" bridge, past a French watertower, a statue of Paul Bunyan (again!), the county buildings. . . .

Seat of the fourth largest county in the state, its name is a French version of an Indian tongue-twister, Unamanitigong. All *that* means is "red."

Manistique owes its history to lumber (twenty mills at one long-past time) and a slice of fame to an odd bridge. As you drive across it looks like any other bridge-road except for solid concrete walls instead of railings on each side. Peer over the walls and you will see that your feet are lower than the surface of the water. The "bridge," in other words, does not arc over the stream but cuts across the top like a cement ditch—"Believe It Or Not," as Mr. Robert Ripley used to go around saying. In fact, the Manistique Bridge was written up in Ripley's newspaper series, a forerunner of the Guinness Book of Records. Its "siphon" tag, however, is a mild misnomer. The water is not siphoned (drawn or sucked) under, but speeds up as it flows beneath the bridge . . . a phenomenon called the "venturi effect" by physicists. The Venturi Bridge? Too late now; anyway, all this does not excite the average visitor as much as knowing that the Manistique River contains some of the best steelhead and salmon fishing in Michigan.

For fishing facts and area information, step to the regal-looking structure next to the bridge, Manistique's Chamber of Commerce. A water tower at one time, the graceful piece of French design is undergoing repairs in the hope that someday visitors will be able to climb to the top.

On the same bit of property is the eight-foot clone of Paul Bunyan (a little shorter than Paul was supposed to be), plus one of the state's tiniest historical museums, a quaint little red farmhouse called the Imogene Herbert Museum. Filled to stove-pipe level with old irons, dishes, pictures, and bric-a-brac. Open summers, uncertain hours.

Visitors are welcome to explore the Wyman Nursery, a tree farm on the north side of town run by the Michigan Conservation Department, complete with park and picnic area along the Indian River.

If you walk out on the breakwater (watch that broken concrete) and stare south, you are looking at 300 miles of water with Chicago the next stop. Manistique's Harbor of Refuge facilities include fuel, electricity, showers, dock attendant, and holding tank pump-out. 906/341-6841. VHF-FM and CB radio.

In August Manistique hosts the Schoolcraft County Fair.

For more Manistique information: Chamber of Commerce, Manistique, Michigan 49854. 906/341-5010.

INDIAN LAKE STATE PARK • West of Manistique, about four miles down Co. 442, this park has 300 campsites, on 567 lovely acres, and an Indian Museum to remind you of who camped here first. Beads and birchbark, lore and artifacts of Michigan's Ottawas, Ojibwas, and others. Mile-long sand beach; good to excellent fishing for bass, bluegills, perch, walleyes. Interpretative center, hiking trails, full facilities.

PALMS BOOK STATE PARK • On the west side of Indian Lake, a fascinating geological extra: Kitch-iti-ki-pi, the big spring that sends 10,000 gallons of crystal-clear water per minute into a pool 200 feet wide and spookily deep. A rope with a raft attached lets visitors pull themselves along, usually dropping coins as they cross in order to watch them flicker like falling stars on their way down.

No camping; just tranquility.

THOMPSON STATE FISH HATCHERY • Back on U.S. 2, not far west of Manistique city limits. Thompson's research helped pioneer Michigan's coho program and the planting of a zillion fingerlings in state streams. Picnic area close by.

It would be possible to take Co. P435 south into the Garden peninsula, but the road does not go near the water, most of the land is private property, and it's easy to get lost. So stick to U.S. 2 and turn south at the sign to Fayette (Co. 483).

FAYETTE–FAYETTE STATE PARK • You'll pass some of the best farms in the Upper Peninsula, the community of Garden, and seemingly endless turns, but about fifteen miles south of U.S. 2 carefully preserved Fayette sits waiting in its own time warp, a vision of things past. The prettiest ghost town in the country, the village occupies a tiny peninsula straight out of a movie set. High white cliffs in the background; a clear blue minisized harbor surrounded by thick trees and gray build-

ings. The shell of a foundry and charcoal kilns look like parts of an ancient castle. There's an opera house, homes, boarding house, and blacksmith's to be peered into on self-guided tours, and an extensive model at the Visitor's Center explaining everything.

Fayette's iron smelting operation prospered between 1867 and 1891. The somewhat ideal company town faded quickly with the advent of more efficient ways of making pig iron, and the railroads shifted such industry to Cleveland and Pittsburgh.

Boaters coming in from Big Bay De Noc will find about six places to tie up, with *no* marina facilities, and must get permission from the park office to stay overnight. The total area of the town-site, park and all, comes to 365 acres, with eighty campsites with electricity, swimming, hiking, and boating.

Fayette is an absolutely *don't miss* spot.

Fayette ghost town

PORTAGE BAY
CAMPGROUND
• Back up from the park about three miles to an intersection called Devil's Corner, take Portage Bay Road (Co. 483 turns, Portage Bay Road goes straight on) to campgrounds on the east side of Garden Peninsula. Eighteen sites, boat launch, campstoves, water, and so forth.

Hiking trails crisscross the southern tip of the peninsula, and will take you to Point De Tour. Supplies at Fairport.

Back to U.S. 2 to continue your drive around the long blue edge.

BOAT LAUNCH
• On the Little Fish Dam River and Big Bay De Noc. Paved ramp suitable for all trailerable boats.

From Isabella or from Nahma Junction, county roads lead south to Nahama, a one-mill lumber town in earlier days. No park, but some lovely bayside places to sit or walk.

FLOWING WELL
CAMPGROUND
• Three miles north of Nahma Junction on U.S.F.S. 13, a dozen campsites, picnic area, water, stoves, and good stream fishing.

FOREST SERVICE
• REST AREA At junction of U.S. 2 and U.S.F.S. 2233.

BOAT LAUNCH
• Paved ramp, but launching of largest watercraft may be difficult. Co. 503 south from U.S. 2, about a mile west of U.S.F.S. rest area.

To explore the Stonington Peninsula, that wide "thumb" separating Big from Little Bay De Noc, take Co. 503 (as directed above) or Co. 513, two miles west of Ensign, making connections via Co. 511. On the west shore road Twin Springs Park offers a bayside picnic place; farther down a Swedish Church and a Norwegian Church loudly hint about the area's settling. The Forest Service maintains a picnic ground near the old lighthouse at Peninsula Point. A marvelous tangle of hiking trails goes through the whole region.

RAPID RIVER
• The intersection of U.S. 2 and U.S. 41 plus H. 05 make Rapid River a literal crossroads of the Upper Peninsula, which is nothing very new. A marker indicates that this was on an old Noc Indian trail between Lakes Superior and Michigan. One of the U.P.'s 150 wa-

140

terfalls can be seen in Rapid River Falls Park where picnic facilities make you want to hang around.

● GLADSTONE

A surveyor named W. D. Washburn came in 1887, exploring locations along the bay with an eye to establishing a railroad center, some place to connect with the Soo, Chicago, and points on the Great Lakes. Thus was founded Gladstone, planned and platted by Washburn and named after the Prime Minister of England. Prosperity came early with lumber and midwest grain shipments, but Gladstone's big industry today is recreation.

Van Cleve City Park overlooks the bay and offers a beach house for swimmers. Three boat-launching points, including the one at the park, are easy to find.

Gladstone's municipal docks have room for eight transients, with gasoline, water, electricity, restrooms, and dock attendant. 906/428-9924.

For summer fun: 10,000-meter Run in July, plus grand and glorious Fourth celebrations.

Eighty campsites are available at the waterside Wilderness Park on the south edge of town. Modern facilities for those who want to swim, water ski, or picnic; open June 1 to Labor Day.

● PIONEER TRAIL PARK

On the Escanaba River north of town off U.S. 2 and U.S. 41; 52 campsites, stoves, showers, playground, and recreation area.

● ESCANABA

Taken from the Indian word "Eshkonabang," which some say is a reference to the red deer available in this happy hunting ground, and others insist is a term meaning "flat rock"—the Indian campsite along the Escanaba River. Whatever, Escanabans with grand pride call their town the "Riviera of the North," having seen prosperity come and go and edge back again, fortunes rising and falling with the course of the mining industries, lumber, grain shipments, and such.

Incorporated as a city in 1883 (one of the youngest cities of its size in the state), "Escie" is not only the county seat but acts as the fun-and-information capital for the whole territory.

The Delta County Historical Museum is small but loaded with Indian and early settler artifacts, and is open from mid-May until Labor Day.

The citizens are justifiably doting over their William Bonifas Fine Arts Center, housing a 365-seat theater for community theater group productions. There's also a gallery for art exhibits, and classes in a variety of crafts.

They might run a little short of the seventy-six-trombone ideal, but over in Ludington Park summer band concerts are fun and spirit-lifting. Tennis courts, picnic areas, and the fishing works besides.

As befitting its regional leadership, the Upper Peninsula State Fair is Escanaba's big summer show, held in mid-August. The C. W. Stoll Yacht Race is a June feature; the Waterfront Art Fair, Venetian Night Festival, and U.P. Steam and Gas Engine Show are August happenings. Write to the Delta County Chamber of Commerce for complete details: 230 Ludington Street, Escanaba, Michigan 49829. 906/786-2192.

Escanaba's Yacht Harbor offers sixteen transient accommodations, and has gasoline, utilities, dock attendant, haul-out, and pump-out. 906/786-9614.

The Minneapolis Shoal Lighthouse in Green Bay between Escanaba and Washington Island was manned until 1978, but is now just a beacon that appears to be built in the water.

A United States Forest Service office is on the north side of the city on U.S. 41 and U.S. 2, 906/786-4062.

The Department of Natural Resources District Headquarters is on M-35, 906/786-2351.

U.S. 2 and U.S. 41 head west; it's M-35 from Escanaba to Menominee.

FORD RIVER BOAT LAUNCH • Paved ramp with lots of parking space. Site of annual August Fish Boil.

FULLER ROADSIDE PARK • Picnic area at the mouth of the Bark River.

J. W. WELLS STATE PARK • Two miles south of the reddish waters of the Cedar River, with over two miles of beach on Green Bay, Wells is a forested sanctuary with all the utilities and additives. Outdoor center, boat launching site, excellent swimming on 974 acres with 155 campsites. Post Office, Cedar River, Michigan 49813. 906/863-9747.

There is no record of what the Menominee Indians said when the • MENOMINEE strange person got out of his canoe, put on a shining robe adorned with feathers, flowers, and birds, and asked to see someone called "Emperor." French voyageur Jean Nicolet was sure he'd find China around here somewhere, but was greeted only by the probably baffled Indians who made gestures about more lands to the west.

Nicolet went no farther; he missed his goal by half a world, although he had quietly opened a land far richer than the Orient.

Menominee (the name means "wild rice") is the Michigan half of the Marinette, Wisconsin–Menominee community that shares the Menominee River mouth on the edge of Green Bay. It's another town with logging tales to tell. In fact, Menominee was the greatest lumbering center of the Upper Peninsula. The first sawmill went up in 1832; in 1893 more than five million feet of logs floated down the river, making it the unofficial world lumbering champion.

Wood and wood products are still part of the local economy, but electrical goods, helicopters, aluminum, and paper products show up well on the charts. Recreation, of course, is a leader since water-bound Menominee is a true gateway-to-vacationland community.

History buffs have two museums to explore. The Menominee County Historical Museum located on Second Street (watch it; they have streets going one way and avenues going the other, a la New York City) and the Marinette County Historical Museum on Stephenson Island (off U.S. 41) both are worth browsing through. The Wisconsin show includes carefully hand-carved miniature logging camps done with rare skill by a local resident. On the Menominee side again, an ill-fated wooden schooner named the *Alvin Clark* is attracting new attention. Called the "Mystery Ship" and carefully chaperoned by its finder, Captain Frank Hoffman, plus a group called the Mystery Ship Preservation Society, the relic has been declared the "oldest documented vessel in existence" by none other than the United States Coast Guard. A grant for restoration funds has been applied for; meanwhile some work is going on and visitors can tour it from mid-June till Labor Day.

Menominee saw Michigan's first highway information center,

where there's a stone said (via Indian legend) to grant special wishes to those who touch it. Make contact before it too becomes a grain of sand.

The Great Lakes Memorial Park and Marina in downtown Menominee sees heavy pleasureboat traffic, and is the site of an annual Blessing of the Watercraft ceremony and numerous yacht races.

Docking accommodations include refueling, water, electricity, showers, pump-out, dock attendant.

Summer specials: Menominee tries to keep things moving with a Fun-o-Rama during the summer months. County Fair time is in late August. For more information, contact Greater Menominee Chamber of Commerce, 1005 Tenth Avenue, Menominee, Michigan 49858. 906/863-2679.

INDIANS IN MICHIGAN

Pottery breaks, wood rots, wampum gets scattered, and legends are vague. Even so, with careful digging and listening to old men's tales we've managed to learn quite a lot about Michigan's early residents. Spear points and broken stone axes in the ashes of a firepit give evidence that humans were in the Detroit area 10,000 years ago. Miners who came from distant places to find copper 5,000 years later left dozens of shallow pits and crude tools. Burial mounds, pottery pieces, piles of grain, and scraps of fabric tell of a complex Indian culture that began around 500 B.C. and lasted a thousand years in what archeologists call the Hopewell Indian period. No one is sure why it died away, but we *do* know that the use of copper was forgotten and the population grew smaller.

In early 1600 when Europeans entered the lakes and woods the principal tribes were the Chippewa, Potawatomi, Ottawa, Miami, Menominee, and Wyandots. The Wyandots were a merger of two Huron tribes and spoke the Iroquoian language; all others spoke a variation of the Algonquin tongue.

Since none of the Indian groups had alphabets or written words, names and meanings were apt to be garbled in the first translations. When someone wrote "Chippewa" someone else read "Ojibwa." These were the tribes of Lake Superior, so spread out they hardly knew they were related until outside pressures made them unite.

Indians had no legalistic absolutes like boundary lines, and it is only possible to give general locations. The Ottawas lived in the northern half of the lower peninsula, mostly along Lake Michigan, while the Miamis occupied the southwest corner of the state along the St. Joseph River. Much of the rest of the southern lower peninsula was Potawatomi territory, except for a water-bound stretch from Lake Erie to the tip of the Thumb occupied by the Huron-Wyandots.

Wyandots built houses sometimes as long as one hundred feet, then divided them into apartments for family units. Nothing was what we would call private, and the smoke from the fires didn't all go through the hole in the roof. We can assume things weren't too comfortable. The other tribes built individual wigwams of bent saplings and bark and lived a slightly different life-style, but all of them used wampum beads strung on deerskin thongs as a money or message exchange, and all of them passed around the calumet (peace pipe) when powwows were held.

There are Indian museums and Indian displays in historical museums to tell you more about how and where they lived, what they wore, how they farmed and fished or hunted. At Cross Village, Indian Lake (U.P.), Mackinaw City, St. Ignace, and Detroit (adjacent to the Fort Wayne Military Museum) you'll find displays plus pamphlets and books on Indians, past and present.

Glance at the map—Keweenaw, Saginaw, Tecumseh, Pontiac, Washtenaw, Kalamazoo, Muskegon, Algonac—and start counting Indian names. Their imprint is upon us; get to know them better.

Isle Royale National Park

EAGLE HARBOR   COPPER HARBOR

CALUMET
HANCOCK   HUBBELL
HOUGHTON   LAKE LINDEN
CHASSELL   JACOBSVILLE

ONTONAGON   BARAGA   L'ANSE
GREENLAND   MARQUETTE
    NEGAUNEE   Pictured Rocks
ALBERTA   Nat. Lakeshore   GRAND   WHITEFISH POINT
    MARAIS   PARADISE
ISHPEMING   CHRISTMAS
    AU TRAIN   MUNISING   SAULT STE. MARIE

PART FOUR

LAKE SUPERIOR

SAULT STE. MARIE TO MUNISING;
CHRISTMAS TO L'ANSE; BARAGA TO WISCONSIN

By the shores of Gitchee Gumee
By the shining Big-Sea Water,
Stood the wigwam of Nokomis,
Daughter of the Moon, Nokomis.
Dark behind it rose the forest,
Rose the dark and gloomy pine trees,
Rose the firs with cones upon them;
Bright before it beat the water,
Beat the shining Big-Sea Water ...

Song of Hiawatha—Longfellow

LAKE SUPERIOR STATISTICS

Length	350 miles
Breadth	160 miles
Length of coastline including Canada and islands	2,730 miles
Total water surface	31,700 square miles
United States surface	20,600 square miles
Total land drainage basin	49,300 square miles
United States drainage	16,900 square miles
Maximum depth	1,333 feet
Average depth	489 feet
Volume of water	2,935 cubic miles

LAKE SUPERIOR

S OME day a very original writer may break the Hiawatha habit and describe Lake Superior without a single reference to "Gitchee Gumee." But why try? To those who are familiar with the lines and have stood on Superior's awesome shores, the poet's vision catches the lake-mood to perfection. Even the cadence of the waves comes through—sounds of a shining sea that still beats against backgrounds of pine; a magnet still drawing wigwams (in the shape of trailers and nylon tents) to its shores.

This is most certainly the Queen of Lakes. A quarter-mile deep, bigger than twelve different states, a force that tells the weather what to do.

Etieene Brule, a rough Frenchman who took to the wilderness and smoke-filled lodges of the Hurons with great zest, was the first European to go along Superior's shores, followed by missionaries and voyageurs.

What the western end of the lake was like—or whether it just went on like an ocean—was unknown even to the Indians at the Soo. Exploring priests and fur hunters pushed westward along a temperamental coast, suffering heat, ice, flies, swift storms, and food shortages; occasionally a few made notes on the magnificent sand dunes and scenic cliffs. The stories of Allouez, Baraga, and Marquette will go down in the annals of tough traveling.

Close to four centuries later a conveyor belt of ships from around the world moves across the big sea to Marquette, Duluth, and Thunder Bay to pick up cargoes of grain and ore. Lands once blasted in Congress by Henry Clay as not worth the expensive locks at Sault Ste. Marie because they were "beyond the moon" are of large importance to the entire globe.

Although upper Michigan saw settlements before the lower part of the state, it was near-total wilderness until the discovery of copper in the Keweenaw peninsula and Ontonagon areas, and of iron in Negaunee ... all in the 1830s. The big boom days were on.

Iron mining continues to be profitable (thanks to new technology), but the rich veins of copper are long gone. The recreational value of Superior lands, however, is pure gold ... especially to those who use vacations as a time for personal quests. There are good restaurants here and there, and a smattering of night life. You can shop, play golf, bowl, listen to jazz—all those relaxations—but the reason for coming is the pull of the outdoors. It's a chance to climb over rocks, explore ghost towns, hike through the forests, or fish the deep ponds. Nothing washes away fatigue like the sight of a waterfall tumbling toward the next stretch of gleaming stream.

Swimming in Lake Superior may lure hardier types who can postpone turning blue, but the most popular waterfront occupations are fishing, agate hunting, and a late-comer, scuba diving. Learn to recognize semiprecious stones in their unpolished state and you begin to understand why so many people spend hours bent like rice planters. Once hooked, it is hard to stand up straight lest a jewel be missed.

Diving grows more popular each year in spite of the cold, hazardous water. Over 500 vessels have gone down in this unpredictable lake where fresh-water depths tend to hold and preserve bodies as well as ships.

Salmon, steelhead, lake trout, and the famous Lake Superior whitefish are the sought-after game; deep-lake charter boats are available all along the coast. In mid-season, however, reservations must be made in advance.

Write to the Upper Peninsula Travel and Recreation Association, P.O. Box 400, Iron Mountain, Michigan 49801, for information.

The shining Big-Sea Water will weave you into a legend of your own.

SAULT STE. MARIE
TO MUNISING

NOBODY in Michigan calls it anything but "The Soo," a word
synonomous with "gateway," "locks," and "busy." If the highest building in Michigan—Detroit's seventy-two-story Westin
Hotel (née Plaza)—were turned on its side and floated into position, it would be considerably shorter than most of the ships
going through the Soo lock system, a necessity caused by the
twenty-one-foot whitewater drop in the St. Mary's River. Visitors
standing on two-story observation decks watch big freighters
squeeze past gates only inches wider than they are (and missing
every time! A wonder to anyone who has ever scraped the garage
door.), then go up or down like corks in a sink. You can observe
the smallest details of the deck gear, and even make eye-contact
with the crew. Just beyond arm's length are lakers and salties from
ports as far away as Tokyo or Liberia. Only winter ends the action.

A scale model in the Visitor's Center shows how the locks work,
how water seeking its own level does the job without the aid of
pumping engines.

The famous Welch Lock Tours operates from two nearby docks,
with two-hour boat rides through a lock, past the Canadian Algoma steel mills and the Canadian Soo, then back through a return
lock. A great trip at $5.00 for adults, half that for children over
six.

Next to the tour docks is the berth of the S.S. *Valley Camp*.
Considered too small for today's shipping requirements, the
550-foot freighter has been turned into a Great Lakes Marine Museum. Visitors go from wheelhouse to hold, and even have a chance

Going through the locks

to examine a battered lifeboat from the tragic *Edmund Fitzgerald*. The Great Lakes Hall of Fame is the adjoining exhibit with a who's who approach.

Two blocks away the Tower of History's brochure says "Walk or ride up 21 stories into Michigan's azure sky." Those who walk are in a sharp minority. The Tower is a concrete eagle's nest for enclosed and unenclosed viewing of the whole locks area. The story of the Jesuit priests who came here first is told via tapes and a minimuseum, answering a few background questions.

If you're still not satisfied, try the Chippewa County Historical Museum (John Johnson house), 906/632-6255, or the Great Lakes Shipwreck Historical Society c/o the *Valley Camp*.

Another way to see things is via the Soo Locks Tractor Train, which starts out from a "depot" directly across from the locks. It ambles across the International Bridge, past historic sites and scenic views. Adults $2.50, children $1.25 for the tour.

The Chamber of Commerce on West Portage Street should be consulted for local information, but don't neglect the bulletin boards of Lake Superior State College, up on the hill. A modestly growing institution, there are events in the new field house that might interest you.

The Soo's Harbor of Refuge offers transient accommodations, gasoline, water, electricity, restrooms, attendant, pump-out. 906/632-9123.

For special summer fun, try the North Country Craftsmen's Art Festival, Twin City International Festival, both in July, or the Sault Summer Arts Festival in August.

One more suggestion: even if you're not planning to travel through Canada, pay a visit to the "other" Soo across the border. Inquire about the wonderfully scenic Algoma Central Railway trip to Agawa Canyon for a one- or two-day treat. Bridge fare: $1.50 for car and passengers.

On the west side of Sault Ste. Marie, a small picnic park near the waterworks. ● SHERMAN PARK

A section of state forest borders this wide inlet but with only dirt roads, and no facilities are available. ● IZAAK WALTON BAY (Mosquito Bay)

153

BRIMLEY STATE PARK • You can stare across the widening St. Mary's River to the rugged Canadian hills from this park, a well-equipped location on White-fish Bay. There are 270 campsites on 151 acres. No park store, but the hiking and fishing are tops.

SCENIC TURNOUT • You are now traveling along U.S.F.S. 3150. Shortly past Bay Mills, look for U.S.F.S. 3151 (gravel) and follow it for about a mile to a scenic turnout on Spectacle Lake. There's also an old cemetery, Mission Hill, close by on the west side of the road.

MIDDLE LAKE CAMPGROUND • U.S.F.S. campsite on Monocle Lake. Close after U.S.F.S. 3151, turn left off of 3150 onto 3699. Minimum facilities.

POINT IROQUOIS LIGHTHOUSE • Boarded up as of this writing, but a very photogenic structure in a lovely spot. No additives for picnickers, although anyone who wants to spread a blanket on the beach and watch the long ships pass is welcome.

INDIAN CEMETERY • Enclosed by a picket fence, you can still visually visit the small "houses" built over the graves. You are asked not to enter; a request that demands respect. These are sacred grounds.

BIG PINE PICNIC GROUND • Under the auspices of the U.S. Forest Service overlooking White-fish Bay.

BAY VIEW CAMPGROUND • Facing the big breezes off Whitefish Bay, the beach is a mix of interesting smooth stones and plenty of sand. U.S.F.S.

TROUT REARING STATION • A U.S. Fish and Wildlife operation, Pendills Creek station. Turn left on U.S.F.S. 3157.

Back to 3150, a scenic serene drive west to M-123.

TAHQUAMENON BAY ACCESS SITE • A hard-surface ramp, suitable for most boats. State park vehicle permit required, as it is about two miles south of . . .

TAHQUAMENON STATE PARK RIVERMOUTH CAMPGROUNDS • Canoeing, excellent fishing, swimming (brr-rr-rr), and 136 camp-sites within easy reach of one of the state's outstanding splendors, Tahquamenon Falls.

PARADISE • The little town with the heavenly name has half-a-dozen resorts, a couple of good hearty-type restaurants, and is the area's general

Tahquamenon Falls

155

social center. If you are determined to stick right to the coast you'll at least make a detour here to see the second largest waterfall east of the Mississippi before heading up toward Whitefish point, and beyond. Most travelers take M-123 to H. 37, and continue their shoreline explorations from there.

At Paradise information is available on local agate hunting, on shipwrecks for scuba divers to see, on berry-picking, and more.

TAHQUAMENON • A roaring tea-colored cascade amid some of the tallest timber and
FALLS STATE PARK the best fishing-stream county in the Upper Peninsula.

The waterfall, colored by tamarack and mineral elements, faces the east and photographers would do well to arrive in the early hours of the day. A huge, 21,137-acre blue-green domain, the park encloses everything except a swimming beach. Hiking through these woods with their well-marked trails (with flora descriptions) is superb. Full facilities for its 319 campsites.

SHELLDRAKE • The highway as it continues north of Paradise is called Wire Road, and if you look hard to the right just as you drive over the Shelldrake River Bridge you can still see a few shabby ruins of a once-busy lumbering community, now one of the U.P.'s ghost towns.

ANDRUS LAKE • Shortly past Shelldrake, turn left toward Andrus Lake and a State Forest campground. Twenty-five sites, good swimming; the best catch is trout.

SHELLDRAKE DAM • Another mile further inland from Andrus Lake and just off Vermilion Road, the seventeen-site forest campground offers good pike fishing but is not recommended for swimming.

WHITEFISH POINT • A boat launching ramp, and a fine place to try some perch fishing from the cement sea wall. The Harbor of Refuge has limited space for transients, with gasoline and water. Brown's fisheries located here is one of the oldest fish industries on the lake.

WHITEFISH POINT • Wire Road dead-ends at the light, now a National Historic site. It's
LIGHTHOUSE time to stop awhile anyway, and walk around the legend-filled point—the wide sandy beach known to the campfires of Indians, voyageurs, and Jesuit missionaries, the silent witness to dozens of

tragic shipwrecks. The light began operating in 1849, making it the oldest active lighthouse on Lake Superior, although the present tower was built much later.

The *Edmund Fitzgerald* and other wrecks have now been visited by famed oceanographer Jacques Costeau who joins the ranks of "salties" with a new respect for the powers of the Great Lakes.

Beachcombing, agate hunting, and building sand castles while the long ships pass on the horizon are the point's priceless offerings. No further facilities.

There are some very poor dirt roads to the shore west of the VERMILION POINT Whitefish Point Light, but to visit Vermilion and the Life Saving Station (no longer active but still maintained), follow Vermilion Road past Shelldrake dam. It's about eighteen miles round trip from the Wire Road intersection.

Keep an eye out for blueberries in these areas!

You *can* follow within a short mile or two along the coast; however, it is not advised unless you have four-wheel drive and are experienced on old logging roads. Return to M-123, go west past Tahquamenon State Park to Northwestern Road (Co. 500).

WHAT'S A PASTY?

There's nothing nasty about a pasty but the sour little adjective *does* remind you how to pronounce the Cornish word for pie. Pasties are the great Upper Peninsula traditional meal, introduced by the miners of Cornwall who came to dig copper during the last century. While recipes are never twice the same, the basic pasty consists of meat, diced potatoes, carrots, onions, and spices placed on a circle of pie dough which is then folded over the contents and baked. Wrapped carefully and inserted under a shirt, the pie stayed warm and kept the miner warm till lunch.

Church bazaars like to sell pasties; Madelyn's, a famed pasty-baking firm in Ishpeming, makes thousands of them a day, and most restaurants have pasties on the menu. Order a tall glass of something cool to go with it, however; they are apt to be a little dry for down-state tastes and very hot.

LITTLE LAKE ● Lake Superior Harbor of Refuge with five transient accommodations, pay telephone, gasoline, electricity, dock attendant, pumpout, restrooms, but no haul-out or repair services. Boat launching ramp and camping are nearby at Bodi Lake or Culhane State Forest campgrounds. A pleasantly isolated spot, twenty-five miles from the nearest restaurant. Come prepared.

TWO HEARTED RIVER STATE FOREST CAMPGROUND ● Thirty-five miles northeast of Newberry via M-123, county roads 500, 414, 412, and 423. In other words, you could easily get lost, but there are forty-five sites and excellent fishing and rock hunting if you persevere.

County roads 410 and 412 wind endlessly through the Lake Superior State Forest, inducing the first-timer to conclude that there is no way out. Continue west, however, and you'll reach Co. 407, paved, the road leading to Muskallonge State Park.

MUSKALLONGE STATE PARK ● On the north side of the large inland Muskallonge Lake, the park also sits on the Lake Superior shore. Called a treasure trove for hunting semiprecious gems, the beach is not for most swimmers. But it provides excellent fishing in a prime wilderness area. For 176 campsites, there are full facilities on 217 acres of park.

BLIND SUCKER FLOODING ● Several state forest campgrounds in close proximity, five to six miles west of the state park. Blind Sucker campgrounds (couldn't they have found a more savory name?) No. 1 and No. 2 are fourteen to sixteen miles east of Grand Marais on Grand Marais Truck Trail, with forty-nine campsites altogether. Another spot on the big lake has eighteen sites and more good agate hunting. Swimming is mostly sandy and *quite* cold.

GRAND MARAIS ● A town so petite that—as one writer was inspired to comment— you can drive through in six heartbeats. A steady population of 450, it has accommodations for nearly 250 vacationers and a tranquil beauty you won't forget. The small harbor has known enough Michigan history to warrant a special preservation designation; from explorers, fishermen, lumbermen, miners, and fur traders to present-day sailors for whom it is a Harbor of Refuge.

158

The inlet is too small for today's freighters, but to the French voyageurs seeking canoe refuge from Lake Superior's storms it was "Voila, le Grand Marais"—therefore one of the first-named places on Michigan maps.

A lighthouse stands at the mouth of the harbor; a park, a dock, and a few visible buildings back of the shoreline road add up to a picture of serenity. In its 1890 heyday, however, Grand Marais had nearly thirty saloons, two newspapers, and a dozen hotels and boarding houses. When the Alger-Smith lumber company closed its mill and the train stopped coming from Marquette, the big time was over.

Anyone who wants to delve into the history of the lakes will find a gold mine in tales of Grand Marais, now the eastern gateway to the Pictured Rocks National Lakeshore.

For boaters there are ten transient accommodations, gasoline and diesel fuel, water, electricity, pump-out, and dock attendant.

Woodland Township Park on Lake Superior has 100 campsites, showers, dumping station, electricity, and the rest. Along with the fishing, swimming, hiking, and agate hunting in such generous supply, there are tennis courts and a children's playground.

Just to see these splendid dunes, these legendary cliffs, is worth all and any effort to get here. That there happens to be fishing, swimming, and other activities dear to a vacationer's heart is a mere bonus; the real thrill is the feast of beauty: the entrancing spectacle of our shoreline treasure. Words like "majestic" and "powerful" aren't enough.

• PICTURED ROCKS
NATIONAL
LAKESHORE

The Grand Sable Banks are glacial deposits rising as high as 275 feet above the lake. Perched on top of the banks are enormous amounts of sand, rising another 85 feet and covering an area at the eastern end of Pictured Rocks of about five square miles. The view up from the water's edge is astounding.

The middle stretch of the lakeshore, called twelve-mile beach, is the shore of Gitchee Gumee as Hiawatha knew it. Thick forests of tamarack, birch, pine, and mixed northern hardwoods are edged by sand, a thick concentration of smooth pebbles, and the cold, blue horizons of a moody lake.

Grand Sable Dunes

Waves and ice have carved the western reaches of the shore, now vertical and hard to see except for the water, into a fantasy of rock caves, arches, and columns. The Pictured Rocks, which rise abruptly as high as 200 feet from the water, glint with the many colors of their mineral composition in the late-day sun.

A *short* distance inland from this varied coast are waterfalls, ponds, streams, bogs, and a feeling of remoteness . . . which is the whole wilderness-preservation idea.

Some highlights of the park:

SABLE FALLS • Tucked behind the dunes near the highway about a mile west of Grand Marais are these splendid falls. There are sturdy steps and railings and great places to photograph the tiers of rushing water, plus a walking trail leading to the top of the dunes and a magnificent view of Lake Superior.

LOG SLIDE • A spot where lumber went into the water the quick way . . . and another breathtaking view. It's also a good take-off place for a hike to the old Coast Guard Station and lighthouse on Au Sable Point. (For a shorter hike, take the path from the Hurricane River campground.)

MINERS • A pinnacle of sandstone eroded into a turret shape, this is one of CASTLE the rock formations that can be seen from shore.

In a scenic, tree-filled canyon the water spills from the center of a high horseshoe-curved cliff into a rushing stream. You can walk under these falls with ease. For the very best of lighting, go late in the day when the sun lights up the sides and back of this west-facing beauty spot.

Munising Falls

161

At the Visitors Center maps and leaflets are loaded with valuable information on the flora, fauna, and camping opportunities. Four campgrounds are listed; backcountry camping is allowed in many remote areas of the park with the proper permit.

For more information write: Pictured Rock National Lakeshore, Munising, Michigan 49862.

MUNISING ● Long before the first voyageur paddled his canoe past Pictured Rocks and opened new shores to the white man's future, Munising was a Chippewa campsite where Daughter of the Moon, Nokomis, cared for little Hiawatha. It's a particularly pretty location in a green half-bowl of rock and pine facing the blue bay. These hills spill over with waterfalls, even within the city limits. Wagner, Tannery, Miner's, and Munising Falls are all only steps from the parking lot.

In the early half of the century when pleasure ships were cruising the lakes, the school band and half the town would come down to welcome strangers. Now the coming and going of visitors on the popular Pictured Rocks tour boats draws little attention. When weather permits, sightseers are taken five times a day during July and August for an otherwise-impossible look at the caves and cliffs of the dramatic coast. Reduced schedule during the last weeks of June, September, and during the color show. Dock at City Pier, 906/387-2379.

For insights into Munising and Alger County history, inspect the Alger County Historical Museum at 203 W. Onota Street. They'll tell you about the Fur Trader's cabin nearby and/or Munising's Victorian City Hall.

The off-shore land mass is Grand Island, second largest in the lake after Isle Royale, and site of some good hiking trails plus an old lighthouse.

The new Alger Underwater Preserve will be moving from proposal to reality even as does this book. Boundaries extend from Au Train to Au Sable Point. Thirteen sites offer divers views of colorful rocks, sunken ships (the *Drednaught*, *Smith Moore*, *Herman Hettler*, *Kiowa*, and others), and underwater caves. Rules and maps are available at the Travel Information Center.

At least six transients at a time can tie up to the Munising Harbor of Refuge docks to find electricity, restrooms, tank pump-out, and attendant. The telephone is a pay station.

Whether you come sailing in on a raft or down the road pulling a swank trailer, you're going to get a warm welcome. Just no brass band.

Munising Chamber of Commerce, 906/387-2138.

A panoramic view plus picnic tables off M-28 just west of town. ●GRAND ISLAND HARBOR OVERLOOK

Three miles beyond the city limits on Lake Superior. For trailers ●MUNISING TOURIST or tents; campstoves, restrooms, showers, playground, water skiing, PARK and more. Room for seventy families, moderate fee.

THOSE STATELY LIGHTHOUSES

When the first lighthouse on the Great Lakes was built at Buffalo, New York, the need for a system of lights was clearly apparent. In 1823 Congress authorized a light near Ft. Gratiot at the outlet of Lake Huron, and thereafter lighthouse construction flourished along with rising commerce. By 1865 there were ten lights on Lake Huron, twenty-six on Lake Michigan, and fifteen on Lake Superior.

Seul Choix Point

Point Iroquois

In the 1850s practically all lighthouses in the land were refitted with intricately prismed glasses called the Fresnel Lens, an advance that magnified and focused beams of light like never before. The efficiency of the lights went up, but so did the costs, and attempts had to be made to economize elsewhere. Sperm oil, used in the big lamps, had risen to $1.64 a gallon, so scientists were asked to test other, cheaper sources. For a while lard oil seemed to be the answer. Then (after a few discouraging explosions) mineral oil or kerosene fed the beam.

Massive formations of ice pushed by currents against the base of lighthouses was a major construction problem; where the building of a tower was not feasible, light*ships* were maintained. One such ship is now a museum, on view in Port Huron.

Harsh, tedious, and isolated, life at a lighthouse could be lonely and especially hard on families. Members of the Lighthouse Service had to keep their wicks in trim, their lights burning without a pause from dusk till dawn, their premises clean, in repair, and ready to receive visitors. However, if everything was kept in top lighthouse shape, special awards and commendations were given.

All the lights on the lakes are now operated electronically, supplemented by rows of harbor lights and buoys that mark the path like the yellow lines on a highway. Most of the grand old towers are in private hands. A few can be visited (Presque Isle, Beaver Island, Copper Harbor, Whitehall) and nearly all of them can be walked around, photographed, and admired. They represent a rugged, legendary tradition; a treasure—public or private—for all.

Manistique

Huron Lightship

CHRISTMAS TO L'ANSE

C AN'T make it through the year without Santa? Collect unusual •CHRISTMAS
postmarks? Here's your break.

Five miles west of Munising on Lake Superior. A daily fee will get •BAY FURNACE
you swimming, campstoves, fishing, and use of boat launch site.   CAMPGROUND
Supplies available at Christmas.

From these sites explore the shore via U.S.F.S. 2491 to Five Mile
Point.

South side of M-28 on Scott Creek.   •SCOTT FALLS

Half-a-dozen tables, four grills on Au Train Bay.   •ROADSIDE PARK

Hard to believe this diminutive community was once the Alger •AU TRAIN
County seat. A very tempting place to stop, especially with small
children in the car who could release energy by splashing around
awhile. The clean beach—crossed by the narrow Au Train River—
has a sand bar that holds the water in a shallow pool long enough
to warm it up. You just don't find this happening much along Lake
Superior.

Check out the hand-squared logs and rough furnishings of the
Charles Paulson house, built in 1883 and restored by the Historical Society. After the history lesson ask about Au Train's charter
boats for some deep-water angling after coho, steelhead, and lake
trout.

You're now in one of the best cabin-renting areas in the U.P.
The Upper Peninsula Travel and Recreation Association has more
details. 906/774-5480.

DEER LAKE SCENIC TURNOUT ● Larger than most roadside parks, and facing a tranquil inland lake, the picnic grounds are still close enough for a walk to the Lake Superior shore.

BAY DE NOC STATE FOREST CAMPGROUND ● This Indian name also appears on northern Lake Michigan shores; you've a right to be confused. Think of the spot as the Laughing Whitefish Campground, which it also is, twelve miles west of Au Train, then two miles north on Campground Road. Fifteen sites, three walk-in sites. Good steelhead fishing in spring and fall plus splendid hiking.

LAUGHING WHITEFISH RIVER ● Lake Superior access site near Deerton has simple gravel ramp, no other facilities. The John Hammer Access, also near Deerton, has a ramp suitable for small to medium boats.

Three scenic turnouts are in a row along the eye-filling, lung-clearing sweep of northern sky and water.

MARQUETTE STATE FISH HATCHERY ● Worth a pause to see how one of our major conservation efforts is operated. Located at 488 Cherry Creek Road. You'll see the sign as M-28 joins U.S. 41 and turns north. 906/249-1611.

MARQUETTE ● It sounds disparaging to say it right out, but as you enter Marquette it will probably not strike you as any great beauty of a town. You either drive under a very utilitarian ore conveyor or swish past masses of roadside emporiums and their competing signs; it's hard to tell which ancient red sandstone structure is "center."

But keep looking. Some of these old buildings (reflected in the walls of shining new ones) are prime examples of their times. There's a lovely row of historic homes along Ridge Street and new neighborhoods glisten in the hills. Follow the streets on the north side of town and you'll reach a curving beachfront near a beautiful peninsula park.

Marquette grew in a valley of rock with a population focused on getting a job done. There was little time wasted on civic prettiness for quite a while. Even now, with public consciousness aroused about such things, Marquette's drawing power comes from a completely unpretentious life-style, infectious energy, and a lot of extra-friendly natives.

The seat of the largest county in the state is *the* shopping center of the Upper Peninsula, the right place to come to find a bargain. Up-and-going Northern Michigan University's campus gives Marquette citizens extra opportunities to enjoy theater, music, and varsity sports. The popular Lakeview Arena swirls with hockey matches, concerts, and conventions.

In the early 1800s Marquette boomed as a lumber center. In those environmentally unconscious years loggers stripped the land of its thick white pine blanket, slowly replaced (after 150 years) with a spread of maple, birch, and hardwoods. The discovery of iron ore in 1844 brought waves of Scandinavian and Italian immigrants whose family names still dominate the phone book. The iron they dug up contributed to the winning of the Civil War and fed the multiple needs of industrialization until the underground veins ran out. Marquette's decline and fall seemed inevitable until the 1950s when a new process for extracting iron from surface ore was made profitable and the community sprang back to life.

(It should be pointed out that the Cleveland-Cliffs Iron Company, open-pit operator and biggest employer in the area, has had an exemplary land policy, giving the public full recreational use of its properties.)

For the vacationer, Marquette has the neat advantage of being an easy part-day drive from everything else in the U.P. plus having plenty to explore right around town.

Absolutely free and fun to watch is the sight of a giant ore ship with its engines stopped a mile out from shore, gliding in toward the loading dock without the aid of tugs . . . a master show of skill. Ship arrival times are in the paper the day before or you can call the Chamber of Commerce, 906/226-6591.

Take a ride on the Marquette & Huron Mountain Railroad, steaming away every summer morning from a bright little depot near the big ore loader. Schedules are subject to change, but between July 1 and Labor Day the genuine four-coacher chugs off on its scenic one-and-a-half-hour run twice a day with a special Lumberjack Breakfast offered on the early train. Reduced schedule in September and during the fall color season. Call the Presque Isle Station, 906/228-8785. Special group rates available. (The Depot restaurant is open most of the year.)

Go slowly around adjacent Presque Isle Park, savoring it from all sides. Walk out on the breakwater only if the waves are not pounding against it (think of the lake as a hungry lion; those cold, high waves have unbelievable and fatal strength). Enjoy the rock formations at Sunset Point and talk to the animals in the small zoo.

The John Burt House, a restored 1858 pioneer workman's cottage, 220 Craig Street, is open daily during July and August, while the Marquette County Historical Museum shows more about the local past, including a life-sized Chippewa diorama. 213 N. Front Street, Marquette, Michigan 49855. Week days 9:00–12:00, 1:00–4:30. 906/226-6821.

Marquette's security state prison has a shop on U.S. 41 where prisoner hobby crafts are sold. Stop and browse, then pull into the Chamber of Commerce office clearly visible on Front Street for a list of motels, restaurants, camp sites, and high lookout points.

They'll remind you not to miss the University's U.P. Sports Hall of Fame, the summer star-gazing programs at Shiras Planetarium, or the tomb of Bishop Baraga in grand old St. Peter's Cathedral.

Summer fun includes the Cliff Ridge Bike Series in June; a bang-

168

up Fourth of July celebration and Art-On-The-Rocks show in July; Rock Swap and Frisbee Competition in August.

The Marquette Harbor of Refuge at Presque Isle has transient accommodations, fuel, water, electricity, restrooms, showers, tank pump-out, dock attendant. 906/288-9866. VHF-FM radio.

● BIG BAY

No road goes completely around the hump of the "rabbit's shoulder," but a detour up to Big Bay has its rewards. On the west shore of the slightly-inland Lake Independence, Big Bay stepped into fame when its hotel was one of the sites used in *The Anatomy of a Murder*. The same hostelry was one of Henry Ford's (the first Henry) favorite retreats, a pillared, frame affair with few pretensions and good food.

Big Bay has a Department of Natural Resources field office and Lake Superior access site with a paved ramp.

The Bay Cliff Health Camp is a large institution (wish there was a better word) for the mentally, physically, and/or otherwise burdened children of the Upper Peninsula; a place for special summer attention and help for problems from reading disabilities to diabetes. If you can arrange a Sunday afternoon visit you'll add a heartening dimension to your trip.

Most of the area beyond Big Bay is private property. Know what you're doing before you go exploring by inquiring at the DNR office for detailed information.

Back to Marquette and U.S. 41.

● NEGAUNEE

Jackson Mine Museum stands on the spot where original mines were worked.

● ISHPEMING

This mining center is known as the cradle of competitive skiing in North America. Watch for signs to Ski Hall of Fame on the north side of the road.

● VAN RIPER STATE PARK

On Lake Michigamme, the park offers an excellent beach, 1,044 acres and 150 campsites.

PARENT LAKE ● ROADSIDE PARK

Fishing and picnicking but no camping.

● CANYON FALLS

On the Sturgeon River it's an easy, delightful hike along a well-

169

marked path from the parking lot. Falls and gorge are especially breath-taking in autumn.

ALBERTA ● Ford Forestry Center shows visitors what the booming sawmill towns of the big logging days were like.

L'ANSE ● At the base of Keweenaw Bay, the entrance to Copper Country. A number of excellent motels and homey eateries make L'Anse a good base for exploring the Huron Bay area, Point Abbaye, ghost towns, and waterfalls. A huge statue and shrine to Bishop Baraga, the pioneer priest who sought his converts on snowshoes and gave the county its name, stands on a sandstone bluff overlooking the bay. Be sure to visit the Baraga County Historical Museum, U.S. 41 Information Center.

The L'Anse harbor has facilities for a few transients and shopping within a block. There is some camping at the Township Park, north of the community on the bay.

Summer fun: Trappers Convention and Bay Shore Run (Pequaming to L'Anse), both in July.

North and *East* from L'Anse:

PEQUAMING ● For a long time, the site of the state's largest ghost town, about eight miles north of L'Anse. Founded as a lumbering operation, it was a typical company operations where houses, stores, and services were all controlled by the owners. In 1887 the population was 700, and twenty-five million feet of lumber were turned out annually. However, the pine eventually ran out, the mill ran down, and the town—headed for oblivion—had one short stretch of revival. Henry Ford wanted to control all the sources of raw material that went into his cars, and so he bought huge holdings in the area, trying to turn Pequaming into a model town. His dream didn't work although today the ghosts have been moved out of spruced-up buildings. Only an old water tower and some memories remain of the past, providing a fascinating story for those who want to dig it up.

SECOND SAND ● On the north side of the tiny Pequaming peninsula, some camping
BEACH PARK available.

Between Keweenaw and Huron bays, a rugged projection that ● POINTE
includes a section of the Baraga State Forest ends at scenic Pointe   ABBAYE
Abbaye. Fine coast for rockhounds.

On Huron Bay, a hard-surface ramp is available but launching and ● SILVER RIVER
retrieving large boats may be a problem. Parking, toilets.   ACCESS SITE

A Huron Bay access not far from Skanee. Paved, heavy-duty ramp ● ARVON TOWNSHIP PARK
and nearby camping.

Campsite in the Baraga State Forest. Fire circles and picnic tables ● BIG ERIC'S BRIDGE
on the sheltered shore of a bubbling Huron River.

In Huron Mountains, Baraga County, the highest point in Michigan: ● MT. CURWOOD
1,996.7 feet.

PUT ROCKS IN YOUR HEAD

Pausing to pick up colorful stones, finding a rock that will look good in the garden or fish tank—it's all part of going to the beach. It can also be the threshold of an addiction known to practitioners as "rockhounding"; collecting stones for their mineral interest or with the thought of making jewelry.

Michigan shores are not exactly strewn with rare gems, but the serious searcher can find agates, jasper, bits of quartz, and frozen colonies of past life such as Petoskey stones. The *un*serious beachcomber will most certainly find enough "pretties" to load the car trunk.

Various booklets try to tell you how to recognize the popular agate in its raw state . . . a stone with soft, translucent swirls that polishes up nicely and makes attractive jewelry. Even in full color such print-and-pic descriptions rarely succeed. Stop at a rock shop, visit some museums, see and handle raw agates, and talk to an expert. *Then* maybe you'll know what you're after, and phrases like "jasper swirls," "scenic cherts," and "porcelain" agates won't sound so formidable.

The Cranbrook Institute of Science, Bloomfield Hills near Detroit, has an outstanding collection of minerals; so does the Seaman Museum at Michigan Technological University at Houghton. Small collections and shops with rock counters are everywhere, with baskets of polished stones and jewelry combining Michigan stones in copper or silver settings.

Just remember, as you meander transfixed by the bounty on the beach, that private property rights go down to the water's edge, regardless of fluctuations in lake level. Obtain the owner's permission or don't trespass . . . or stay where your feet are always wet. If you go digging in quarries or mine dumps you should also make every effort to stay off private land.

The best rock beaches in the state run along the Lake Huron shoreline from Cheboygan to Alpena (there are plenty of public access points), then along the rough shores of Lake Superior, especially the Keweenaw Peninsula and westward to the Wisconsin line. Try McLain State Park or the agate beach between Eagle Harbor and Eagle River.

WHAT ABOUT THE PETOSKEY STONE?

The official Michigan stone is not a true stone but a fossil, a kind of coral, Genus Hexagonaria, fairly common in the Traverse City area. Although many such coral collections are relatively soft, the Petoskey stone is hard enough to take buffing and polishing, which makes it a popular prize.

BARAGA TO WISCONSIN

A s you arc around the southern tip of Keweenaw Bay you are not just entering another region, you are coming into Copper Country ... beautiful, historic, and with a mentality all its own. Old-timers here think in three dimensions: east, west, and down, down, down into the miles of tunnels, shafts, and stopes of the copper mines.

Nearly 5,000 years ago an unknown race of men came long distances to mine the malleable, versatile element in the regions of the Keweenaw. They left hundreds of shallow pits with enough evidence such as stone tools to prove what they were after (but no sign of permanent encampments) and vanished.

Voyageurs and missionaries picked up chunks of red metal but said little. Their souvenirs, however, did not go unnoticed and rumors grew. When geologist and chemist Douglass Houghton said, "Its true. There's copper in those hills," fortune hunters, speculation miners, gamblers, and every breed of red-eyed prospector ever seen in the movies came up, fighting cold, hunger, and Dame Fortune for a chance to dig copper—which the growing legend had thickly laced with silver.

The great rush started six years before the '49ers struck out for California and thirty years ahead of the silver strike in Colorado, and proved to be richer in the long run than either of the others. Somehow this northwoods stampede did not enter the American consciousness the way other metal discoveries have done; it has escaped the national mythology.

Most of the early comers died broke and only a fraction of the mining companies managed to pay dividends, but generally the Keweenaw Peninsula prospered mightily. Nowhere in the world had copper been found in such pure abundance. At the time of the first discovery copper was used mainly for cooking utensils, jewelry, and as sheathing for ships. Its market value rose and fell. However, when the telegraph and other electrical devices came along the value of copper went up a thousandfold. Cornishmen ("Cousin Jacks"), Italians, Finns, Estonians, and a host of others came on ships, mules, and two feet to find jobs in the mines. Calumet grew to be a rich city of 47,000 and for a while was even considered as a possible site for the state capital.

The big payloads are gone now, the shafts capped, and only a few unplanned monuments remain. The big rusting shaft house on Hancock hill is one of them—back roads are dotted with others.

It is a new world in Copper Country with state parks, a state university, an airport with scheduled flights, good roads, and all the additives. Beautiful. Dig in.

BARAGA PLAINS WATERFOWL MANAGEMENT UNIT • Observe the winged comings and goings of Canada geese and migrant ducks as U.S. 41 circles the south end of Keweenaw Bay.

BARAGA STATE PARK • Adjacent to the bird refuge, the park has 137 campsites, swimming (cold!), and a lovely view of the bay. Boat launch, sanitation station, hot showers, and other comforts.

BARAGA • Those mighty-muscled scoops that can pick up half-a-dozen logs or ten boxes of freight at a time, the Pettibone Cary-Lift, are made in Baraga . . . unlikely as that seems. The town is proud of its sturdy local product, winner of Michigan's Product-of-the-Year Award, and of its reputation for community spirit.

Baraga's Department of Natural Resources Field Office will give information on scenic spots and fishing sites. Summer events: Keweenaw Bay Arts Festival in July; Rock Swap and Croatian Festival in August.

A choice detour from here would be to follow M-38 (the road to Ontonagon) to Prickett Dam Road then turn south toward Silver Mountain and the Sturgeon River Falls and Gorge. Sometimes called the "Grand Canyon of Michigan," the Gorge is one of the deepest in the midwest.

On a high bluff overlooking the bay, six miles north of Baraga, ● ROADSIDE PARK with tables, grills, and the contours of the Huron Mountains on the far horizon.

As U.S. 41 enters Houghton County it swings westward toward the peninsula center. Chassell, Houghton, Hancock, and other towns may not seem to be on the long blue edge, but Portage Lake and the Lake Superior Ship Canal effectively turn most of Keweenaw into an off-shore island. This short-cut provided ships with a way to avoid the hazards of traveling around the tip of the rocky region and saved time, but with advances in radar, faster freighters, and the lack of heavy local commerce, Keweenaw Portage use has fallen off sharply.

Will get you out onto Portage Lake. A small ramp for canoes and ● STURGEON RIVER car-top boats.   SLOUGHS ACCESS

Quiet resting spot off U.S. 41, just south of Chassell.   ● ROADSIDE PARK

On Portage Lake tucked away from the main traffic. If you reach ● CHASSELL Chassell in July, hang around for the Strawberry Festival, or pick up a list of U-pick strawberry farms from Copper Country Chamber of Commerce, Portage Avenue, Houghton.

Access site with a paved ramp. The gray "beach" is stamp sand, a ● SUNSHINE BEACH residue from copper mining operations.

The mirror-image hills on which these twin communities are ● HOUGHTON– perched rise sharply from the narrow, river-like west end of Por-   HANCOCK tage Lake as if they were bleachers along a parade route. Pleasure boats, Coast Guard cutters, and occasional freighters pass in review between steep tiers of houses, businesses, churches, trees, and more hills. There's even a triumphal arch: the double-deck hydraulic lift bridge across the water.

Ransom Sheldon and his brother-in-law, Christopher Columbus Douglass, saw nothing man-made when they came to the Keweenaw in the 1840s, but the men shared visions of opportunity. They discovered the Pewabic Amygdaloid Lode and were first to successfully extract copper by "stamping" it from rock that had been scorned as useless. Then the two of them platted Houghton and Hancock (the latter named for the American patriot), sold the first lots, and built houses and the area's first hotel.

Seeing the need to remove sand bars that blocked the mouth of Portage Lake at its Keweenaw Bay entry, the entrepreneurs formed an improvement company to dredge an opening, enabling ships to anchor at the mill-site docks.

Sheldon and Douglass prospered mightily and their names are understandably part of the twin city lexicon.

A fire nearly burned Hancock into oblivion in 1869, but the undaunted population kept growing, bringing railroads and a bridge. As soon as the Ship Canal was constructed (1873) connecting the slender arm of Portage Lake to the west side of the peninsula and Lake Superior, Houghton and Hancock were official big-league ports of call.

The technology of mining also shot ahead from lucky-guess-and-muscle-power beginnings, producing a demand for scientifically trained personnel. Houghton's Michigan Technological University started off as the Michigan School of Mines, just a corner nowadays of a much-expanded arts and business curriculum. The Seaman Minerological Museum in the University's Electrical Energy Resources Center has a 30,000-specimen display of rocks and gemstones. The ultraviolet display is fascinating, even if all you know about rocks would hardly make a paperweight. Open weekdays to the public when school is in session. Call 906/487-2572. No charge.

The only college in America founded by folks from Finland is Suomi in Hancock where the mother tongue still gets major attention. New modern additions are part of the two-year school but Old Main is considered something special for visitors to see. So is the Hancock Fire Station, City Hall, and County Courthouse in Houghton.

If the region has a trademark, an unplanned memorial, it has to be the tall, strangely regal-looking hulk on top of Hancock Hill, Quincy Shaft House No. Two. This rusting sentinel represents one of the most successful of all Copper Country operations, a mine

Quincy Shaft House
No. Two

177

that paid dividends every year from 1867 to 1921. From the structure, the Quincy mine enters the ground and keeps going for 9,260 feet—over a mile and a half into the earth. The enormous hoist needed to lift and lower miners and ore from such a depth (well over the height of seven stacked World Trade Centers or Sears Towers) is a wondrous piece of machinery open to public inspection.

Since the whole Keweenaw Peninsula is close to the "Edge" and no single road goes all the way around, we'll treat this area as though it were all on the waterfront.

HUBBELL–LAKE • You'll find a boat launching site at Hubbell on the west side of
LINDEN Torch Lake. If the lake gives hints of being reddish, it is; unknown tons of copper tailings have been dumped into its waters. Two minutes away is the Hungarian Falls and Dam, a regular Niagara in the springtime. Between Hubbell and Lake Linden the scene includes the bombed-look ruins of Ahmeek Mill, a copper producer. The Houghton County Historical Museum on M-26 at Lake Linden, housed in the former Calumet & Hecla (Ahmeek's owners) offices, can tell more about the mill's origins ... plus others like it.

JACOBSVILLE • Take Bootjack Road from Lake Linden to get to this small community on the Portage entry. Much of the local building material came from the sandstone cliffs you see, and there's a good-size breakwater for shore fishing.

GAY TO LAC LA • Go back to Lake Linden, then follow Co. 562 (Gay Road) to the
BELLE Lake Superior shoreline drive. Several roadside picnic stops on an under-visited section of coast. A Harbor of Refuge can be found by boaters at Grand Traverse Bay (called Big Traverse Bay on some maps). Three transient berths, very limited facilities. If you pull in here it's seven miles by road to the nearest store.

Another refuge, Lac La Belle has a few more transient accommodations, gasoline, and a chance to eat someone else's cooking at pretty little Bete Gris. Instead of turning inland here, follow the road around to the far side till it turns and comes out near the beach—a marvelously fresh spot with sand that "sings" as you walk along. One of the old lighthouses, now privately owned, can be seen at the end of the road.

Back on U.S. 41, a ghost town and place for a mine tour to get • DELAWARE more of the inside story.

U.S. 41 finishes its long course from Florida by winding and turning through a green tunnel on the approach to Copper Harbor. Past the nearly-hidden ghost houses of Mandan, past Lake Medora and a gravel-ramp public access site, past the Keweenaw Mountain Lodge. Stop. The Lodge is a spreading log beauty built by unemployed miners during the Depression as a WPA project. It's one of the rare hostelries owned and operated by a county government, has twenty beautifully modern-but-rustic log cabins at reasonable prices. With a nine-hole golf course, lounge, and excellent food, the lodge rates special notice.

When freighters were smaller and copper was bigger, the eye- • COPPER HARBOR filling little cove called Copper Harbor bustled with commerce. Only its reputation as a beauty spot in a growing recreational area saved it from becoming another ghost town at the end of the line. Stores are full of traditional and local souvenirs; several excellent restaurants and motels are located here. The *Isle Royale Queen* departs for the national park site every morning; reservations must be made. If you miss that boat, ask about the sunset cruises.

The historic lighthouse is now a Marine Museum reached only by a short boat trip from the Copper Harbor marina. It's the perfect spot for photographers, kids, or anyone seeking a breezy place to watch wave action against a rugged shore.

The boat refuge has ten transient berths, gas, water, showers, pump-out, dock attendant, and a telephone number: 906/289-4410. VHF-FM radio.

Built in the mid-1800s to guard copper miners from Indians, but • FORT WILKINS used mostly to guard the miners from each other, restored and   STATE PARK sparkling Fort Wilkins is a giant plus of the 200-acre park. There are 165 campsites beneath the pines on the banks of Lake Fanny Hooe, just steps from the Lake Superior shore.

BROCKWAY • Surely the most scenic piece of pavement in the state, the soaring,
MOUNTAIN DRIVE   dipping, winding drive up to the top is an experience. First you
pause for an overlook of Copper Harbor, then you join the birds
on their way to the summit, 600 feet above the lake; on a clear
day you can see Isle Royale. On any day there are freighters passing way out on the lake, and undulating waves of hills and cliffs
stretching two thirds of the way around. Gift shop for souvenirs
and postcards, but there's little danger of your forgetting the scene.

EAGLE HARBOR • Another mining outlet, now a serene little village with a soft sandy
beach. The Knights of Pythias was founded here. Of interest is the
general store, a real old-timer, and the hiking trails in the surrounding woods. Ask about the trail to Blueberry Hill if you come
in August.

Harbor of Refuge provisions include limited transient berths,

180

attendant, gasoline, water, electricity, showers, pump-out, and the rest. 906/289-4416.

M-26 curves in and out along a rocky boundary that looks to some folks like the coast of Maine. There are bits of beach at Cat Harbor and stonier shores at Great Sand Bay with roadside tables and scenic invitations to stop and enjoy.

The Keweenaw County seat has the oldest courthouse in Michigan. The road bridges over Eagle River Falls, another springtime torrent nearly finished by late summer. A memorial to Douglas Houghton, who lost his life by drowning near Eagle River, can be seen on the west side of town. ● EAGLE RIVER

M-26 then turns toward Phoenix, although a county road continues along the shore, giving you one more roadside park before it also turns inland.

Enrico Caruso sang here; so did Jenny Lind. Sarah Bernhardt and Otis Skinner both paraded their acting skills before Calumet audiences. What brought such luminaries to this decidedly off-track outpost? ● CALUMET

The answer is *money*. Once Calumet was a giddily prosperous city of 47,000 and just a few votes away from becoming the state capital. After a rough start as a hell-bent mining town named Red Jacket, wealth, sobriety, and civic-mindedness took over. It didn't even seem reckless to build the first municipally-owned theater in the United States at a cost of $70,000 (with a capacity of 1,200) or to bring in the glossiest talent money could lure. The Calumet Theater—they called it the Opera House—opened in 1900. John Philip Sousa, Lillian Russell, Houdini. . . .

Calumet went down but it never, however, went out. Travelers will find some good (if basic) restaurants and enough general merchandise to fill shopping needs. An interesting assortment of churches testifies to the stubbornly nonecumenical mind-set of Finns, Italians, Cornishmen, and other immigrant ethnics who once poured in to work the mines.

The theater is no decaying relic. Used quite a lot in recent years and now beautifully restored to its original glory, the building is a source of great Calumet pride. Call or ask about possible programs or to take a building tour, then go down to the theater crowd's favorite after-show spot, Shutes (almost next door), where an antique Tiffany canopy is part of the never-redone decor of the old saloon. Write: Calumet Theater, 6th Street, Calumet, Michigan 49913, or call 906/337-2610.

The Coppertown U.S.A. Museum and Visitors Center in an old Calumet and Helca Company building on Red Jacket Road have changing exhibits of arts, crafts, and mining history: pictures, pick axes, and paraphernalia. Open mid-May until the 1st of October, Tuesday through Friday, 1:00 PM till 4:00 PM. 906/337-1976.

Nearby Laurium, which also had a large theater, is the hometown of Notre Dame's football great, George Gipp. A memorial to the "Gipper" stands in one of the parks. For a mini-industrial tour, drop by the Copper Shop on the main street and watch sheet copper (ironically, ordered from Chicago) turned into colored leaves, ships, and wall decorations with only the application of heat and water.

Off M-26 toward Lake Linden, follow a path to a *deep* gorge, site of the 120-foot Douglas Houghton Falls, highest in the Upper Peninsula. Watch your step; this is a lovely but treacherous spot.

MCLAIN STATE • On Lake Superior, only minutes from Hancock, McLain has a long, PARK beautiful beach and plenty of room. Ninety campsites (that lake wind, straight from the Arctic, can be tough on tenters) on 401 acres of park; it also faces Bear Lake. Complete facilities except boat launch.

At the north end of the Portage Ship Canal two breakwaters reach out like long arms on both sides of the entrance, a fine place for ship-watchers or someone with a long fishing pole. The U.S. Coast Guard maintains a station on the east (it *is* east at this point) bank and a Harbor of Refuge is just a little further in on the same side. Twenty transient accommodations, gasoline, water, electricity, attendant, haul-out facilities, pump-out, showers, the works. 906/482-5928. VHF-FM radio.

Ten miles from Houghton, with camping, picnic area, bathhouse, • NORTH CANAL
playground, boat launch, and all the rest. No store, however; sup- TOWNSHIP PARK
plies are five miles away.

Also called Agate Beach Park. No road along the lake means you • STANTON
must take M-26 to Toivola and then county roads west to the TOWNSHIP PARK
water's edge. Camping, electricity, water pump, and so forth. You
can swim if you'd like, or even water ski. Boat launch site, community building, playground. For more bread and crackers, go
back to Toivola.

Back inland, M-25 passes **Twin** (Polland and Gerald) **Lakes
State Park** on the way back to Ontonagon and the shore. There
are sixty-two campsites in the heavily wooded hills; swimming
and good fishing. See Wyandotte Falls, west of M-26 on county
road, south end of the park line.

Site of the Adventure Copper Mine, open to tours. Another chance • GREENLAND
to see the glowing metal in its rock-bound state. One of the shafts
opens out onto a high scenic lookout so don't leave the camera
in your car.

At the Smithsonian Institution in Washington, D.C., rests a huge • ONTONAGON
chunk of copper known as the *Ontonagon Boulder*, symbolic
perhaps of all the valuable ore that has been taken from this region
for deposit in other places. The boulder once sat in the Ontonagon
River and was considered semisacred by the Ojibways, the folks
who named the town. On-toe-nah-gun means "place of the bowl."
From a mining-lumbering past, Onto-etc. is now the base of a
flourishing paper mill, an interesting operation for summer visitors
who'd like to make an appointment to watch. Call the public
relations office. A conglomerate of odds and interesting ends can
be found at the Ontonagon Historical Museum's extremely casual
exhibit. County Fair time is late August.

The nearby coasts are good places to hunt for mineral and
driftwood specimens; fishing (you can charter deep-lake boats) is
exceptional; smelt dipping runs a little late.

Harbor facilities provide some transient berths, gasoline, water,
electricity, restrooms, showers, attendant, haul-out equipment, and

a pay station telephone. The township park on Lake Superior will accommodate a few campers.

Going *eastward* from Ontonagon not far from the lakeshore, hikers will find an abandoned railroad bed extending for about seven miles, plus trails that will take them to Tenmile Point, the Fourteen Mile Point Lighthouse, and Sleeping Bay.

ROADSIDE PARK ● Westward on M-64, Green Park faces the big lake.

PORCUPINE ● 58,000 acres of ancient mountains, forests, streams, coasts, and MOUNTAINS beauty. At 1,958 feet above sea level, the Porcupine Mountains WILDERNESS STATE are the highest range in mid-America, part of what is known to PARK geologists as the pre-Cambrian shield. In an elaborate trail system that lets you hike for a day or a week, Adirondacks-type shelters are available to those who reserve them in advance, and even cabins with bunks and stoves can be rented. Unless your request for these popular digs is made very early, be prepared with alternate plans.

The Porc Park winter sports area has a handsome ski lodge (no overnighters) and a long, delightful chair lift ride running all summer. Not far away is the single most popular spot for gazing into space in the state; the high lookout point grandly offering eagle views of the Lake of the Clouds and the tree-carpeted hills. Hypnotic.

Along the south boundary road tall stands of virgin pine and hardwood provide an avenue of splendor, with flourishing encores during the fall color show.

Traders Falls, Trappers Falls, Shining Cloud Falls, and the enchanting spills of the Presque Isle River are reasons to wander through the west end of the park pretty thoroughly. It would be a shame to miss any of these ... a short segment of a long list.

Open to hunting in season and always the best of fishing, there are 199 campsites in the park with full facilities.

COPPER PEAK SKI ● On Co. 513 between Bessemer and the park at the mouth of the FLYING HILL Black River stands the highest man-made jump in the Western hemisphere, a giant slide used for world championship meets. By chairlift, elevator, and small fee you can reach the top any summer

U.P. waterfall

day for a magnificent view of forests and lake. Open weekends during the color season.

BLACK RIVER • A Harbor of Refuge, U.S.F.S. campground, and a bonanza of water-
HARBOR falls. Starting across a suspension bridge over the swirling river, hiking is easy going and scenic. Bugs like it too, so pack insect spray and don't use perfumed soaps.

The harbor offers gasoline, water, and restrooms, but that's about all.

LITTLE GIRLS POINT • Limited number of unimproved campsites on Lake Superior. Take Co. 505 (runs just west of Gogebic County Airport). Indian burial mounds are nearby.

ISLE ROYALE • A loon calls; a moose wades into the far side of the lake; wind
NATIONAL PARK swishes like an attending nurse through the pine tops. The stac-
Black River bridge cato of outboards and droning of trail bikes are forbidden on Isle

Royale, the largest island in Superior. You must walk or paddle to inland fishing and camp sites.

It is said that we can thank Ben Franklin, our shrewd ambassador at the Treaty of Paris, for maneuvering an international boundary between Canada and the territories so that the island belonged to the United States. Just what Franklin thought the isle was worth is not clear, but 200 years later it is priceless; a pristine, primitive wilderness where nature is in balance because it has been left alone.

The main island is forty-five miles long and nine miles wide with about 200 islet satellites scattered around the edges. One hundred twenty miles of foot trails lace the woods, giving the avid hiker a chance to wander for days.

The usual mistake of shooting off the predators has not been made on Isle Royale. Moose are kept in check by the meat-hungry wolves; packs of wolves are thinned by the lethal hoofs of the moose. Muskrat, mink and beaver, weasel and fox swim the lakes or dart across the clearings, but deer, skunk, and porcupine are island strangers.

An amazing variety of tiny woodland orchids grow among hardwood and conifer giants. They are only one specie among hundreds of wildflowers. A real botonist's surprise was the discovery of Devil's Club, ordinarily found only in the Pacific Northwest.

The most frequently seen bird is the herring gull, but twenty-five kinds of warblers have been spotted.

Isle Royale's 539,280 acres of deep forest and rugged, rocky shores provide sweeping vistas and heavy doses of serenity. There are campgrounds along the trails and accommodations at the far ends of the isle for seekers of these treasures, but one fascinating aspect of island history is that 3,000 years ago there were other visitors seeking other treasures. Ancient Indian mining pits filled with primitive tools and the charred evidence of fires show that this was a source of copper to men who came, mined, and vanished forever.

More recent relics include the Rock Harbor Lighthouse, built in 1855, and the Windigo Mine, a copper pit mined by white men until the end of the last century.

Rock Harbor Lodge at the north end offers housekeeping rooms and private baths, dining, groceries, snacks, camping and fishing needs ... including canoes for rent. Down at the southern area, the Windigo site has a camp store, sandwiches, limited fishing accessories, gas, boat and motor rentals (for going around the outside and to other islands only).

For reservations and information write to: National Park Concessions, Inc., Rock Harbor Lodge, P.O. Box 405, Houghton, Michigan 49931. 906/482-2890. Because of its remote location, allow extra time for a reply. Winter address (Labor Day to June 1): National Park Concessions, Inc., Mammoth Cave, Kentucky, 42259. 502/758-2217.

On getting there: for information and reservations on the ferry *Ranger 111*, with service from Houghton, write Isle Royale National Park, Box 27, Houghton, Michigan 49931. 906/482-3310. For information and reservations on the *Isle Royale Queen II*, with service from Copper Harbor, write to it as such, zip 49918. Mid-June to September call 906/289-4437; winter (September to mid-June), try 906/482-4950.

To go by seaplane: Isle Royale Seaplane Service (June-August), Box 371, Houghton, Michigan 49931. For winter information (September-March), 18 Airport Road, Shawano, Wisconsin 54166. 715/526-2465.

Note: Days on Isle Royale are cool, nights are cold. Bring your warm underwear and plenty of insect repellent.

THE FOREST PRIMEVAL: MOSTLY PRIME AND SELDOM EVIL

(Regular hunters, campers, etc. are invited to skip this)

"Lions and tigers and bears, Oh My!" In *The Wizard of Oz*, Dorothy and her friends tiptoe nervously through the forest . . . well you know the scene. It reflects part of the universal folklore that deep in the darkest part of the woods lies the dragon's den, the witch's lair, and creatures waiting to gobble you up.

More realistically, shadowy forms in the trees, a few swooshing bats high overhead, and the ease with which one can get lost gives the forest areas an unnerving power, especially as the sun goes down. The city slicker may claim backache problems that won't allow for anything but motel beds, but underneath the real reason for not tenting in the forest is fear. Fear of things that go bump, hoot, and grr-rr in the night.

I'm not about to say "Get out and camp. You don't know what a great experience you're missing!" (if the shoe fits . . .). Here are some hints, however, that should make your daytime woods walking more relaxing and fun.

1. Don't wear perfume, after-shave, scented deodorants, or anything that will make an insect think you're a flower. The scent of human breath is signal enough . . . even through mouthwash and chewing gum. *Do* wear some good commercial bug-shoo.

2. Wear comfortable shoes that can handle squishy spots in the path. Take a sweater, especially if the trail goes in and out of the woods and then along the shore. The differences in temperature can be astonishing.

3. Carry a small nature guidebook to help you tell the trillium from the thimbleberries, and the birches from the tamaracks. In other pockets or your knapsack put a candy bar and flashlight; both will do wonders to ward off panic if you are late getting back.

4. A compass is also basic on anything but very short-trail hikes. Know exactly which direction you're headed when you begin. If you plan to be gone all day, tell someone (motel owner, park ranger).

5. Don't eat the berries or mushrooms unless you're positive you know what you're doing. Some very pretty items can give you an awful ache.

6. Stick to a marked trail. They often seem to zigzag endlessly and you may think you sense a shortcut, but over-confidence is often a part of getting lost.

What if you meet a bear? The Upper Peninsula biggie. You're not likely to, unless you're still hiking after dark. Bears are nocturnal for the most part, and (I too find this hard to believe) are more nervous

about you than you are of them. Copper Country folks just talk louder and wave flashlights if they suspect a bear is nearby.

Keep all food tightly wrapped in foil or tins.

NEVER NEVER NEVER approach a wild animal with food or to pet it. Do not get out of your car to photograph bears.

But *do* keep an eye out for the other forest creatures. Here's a list of some you may see . . . and some you may not.

THE WOLVERINE There is nothing harder to get rid of than a well-established symbol. That means that the reclusive, nasty-tempered wolverine—who doesn't even live here any more—will probably stay in office as the official Michigan animal. Heavily built with shaggy hair, wolverines are of the weasel family, relatives of badgers, otters, skunks, etc. For its size the wolverine is one of the most powerful animals in the world and is known as a vicious fighter who will kill when neither defense nor food is at stake. Now exceedingly rare, three wolverines live well but grumpily in the Detroit Zoo.

RED FOX Not always popular, the fox is credited with unusual wit, agility, and ability to survive. They are burrowers and night hunters, love to dine on birds and eggs, mice, lizards, frogs, and even snakes.

The fox population in Michigan has gone up and down, but seems to be on the increase at this time. Devoted parents, both male and female feed the helpless young and demonstrate rare courage when the pups are threatened.

RACCOONS, BEAVERS, OTTERS, PORCUPINE, SKUNKS . . . all creatures soft or pricky. . . . Michigan woods, ponds, hollow logs, and small caves harbor a varied population of small and busy beasts. Skunks and racoons are most likely to be met after dark; the others are even more elusive. Raccoons are scarce along Lake Superior, and the beaver's seldom seen south of Lansing. Otter, those happy fellows who spend much time sliding down hills for the sheer joy of it, range widely in the upper areas of the state but are extremely difficult to spot. The porcupine (who can*not* throw any quills) ranges through the otter's territory, but you're most apt to find his barbs in Au Sable River country or the woods of Menominee County. Porcs like to chew on oar handles; they're after the salt of human sweat.

The zoo at Clinch Park, Traverse City, is a fine place to pick up Michigan animal facts and figures.

RABBITS What's the leading game animal of Michigan? Peter Cotton-

tail, invader of gardens, appealing hero of children's books. The highly reproductive rabbit will have three or four litters a year; about five blind and helpless young cottontails are in each litter. With speed and astonishing agility they manage to elude enemies, but can deliver hard blows with their back legs when necessary. Rabbits are partial to areas of thick underbrush and like nothing better than a dense patch of woods near an abandoned farm.

The cottontail's first cousin is the snowshoe (or northern jack) rabbit. Bigger, tougher, with wide feet that are well adapted to traveling across the snows of winter, this bunny is not quite so prolific, although it may produce more in one litter. For meals, the snowshoe dines on small shoots and sprigs of the northern forests, with a little bark of birch or willow for dessert.

WHITE TAILED DEER Big, soft brown eyes, intelligent faces, graceful and sleek; the white tailed deer is the most widely distributed big game animal in North America. It thrives in a region of combined woods and open country and was one of the animals to benefit from the thinning out of the Michigan forests.

Those wondrous horns—antlers—on the head of the male are grown anew every year. Their one purpose is to keep the other bucks away from his lady friend and when that's insured, the antlers fall off.

For her part, the doe gives birth to a little spotted fawn or two in May or June.

More than half a million deer hunters go after their piece of venison every fall, bringing home between 60,000 and 120,000 animals. Yet one of the biggest threats to the deer is your car. They haven't learned to read "Deer Crossing" signs, so it's up to you to be alert.

MOOSE AND ELK The moose, monarch of Isle Royale, is an awesome-sized beast with that designed-by-a-committee look. His neck is too short and his legs seem too thin, yet he gets around nimbly and is a great swimmer . . . even with a rack of antlers nearly six feet wide. Those surprising horns, like a deer's, are shed each winter and grown from new nubs the following year. Moose are unpredictable and moody creatures; for a really close-up look, head for the zoo.

Elk, moose, and deer all share the winter practice of staying within one clump of trees, browsing on whatever sprigs and buds they can find. Elk, smaller than the moose, vanished from the state for a time but was reintroduced with seven animals in 1918. The new herd grew to 2,000, then dwindled to a mere yardful. Now protected and again on the increase, your best chance to spot an elk is in the Pigeon River valley of the lower peninsula.

HOW BIG WAS THE FUR BUSINESS?

For more than a century and a half French, British, and independent traders and trappers had been taking the fur bounty of the Michigan area wilderness when *one* company, the Northwest Company, listed this inventory in 1798. It does not, of course, include the animals killed whose skins were deemed too poor in quality to accept.

106,000 beaver skins
2,100 bear skins
1,500 fox skins
4,000 kitt fox skins
17,000 musquash skins
32,000 marten skins
1,800 mink
6,000 lynx
600 wolverine
3,000 wolf
700 elk hides
500 buffalo robes

Total: 175,200 pelts.

Notice that deer skin, so useful to the Indians and pioneers, is not on the list of desired furs. Chief buyers of furs were the courts and aristocrats of Europe, a market that fell abruptly with the 1790s French Revolution, although trapping and trading continued for another score of years.

PART FIVE

FOR YOUR
INFORMATION

A LITTLE LIST OF
FAVORITE PLACES

WHEN asked to recommend motels or restaurants, I usually try to beg off since my tastes yo-yo between grand duchess and peasant, and the amount of cash on hand is never twice the same. Sometimes (after a week of tenting in the rain) I feel the need of a luxury fix, but will more often settle for good coffee and pie served at the counter.

A few places around the state, however, are so memorable that it would be a shame not to comment on them. I won't go heavily into menus or exact street addresses, etc.; they are all easy to find with numbers in the phone book.

The gracious early American ambience of *Dearborn Inn*, across from Greenfield Village, turns me into instant-mellow. Eat here or go to Detroit's *Joe Muer's* for seafood.

In Algonac, on the way to Port Huron, *Henry's* has good family eating next to the water. A bit further up the road the wonderfully romantic *St. Clair Inn* puts dining and overnight guests close to the long ships; the *Fogcutter Restaurant* atop the People's Bank Building in Port Huron gives a lofty seagull's look at river traffic plus class.

Folks buzzing to the Thumb may want to detour to Frankenmuth for a fabulous dinner at *Zender's* or the *Bavarian Inn*. Ach du lieber!

Leaping up to Harrisville, the small *Big Paw Resort*'s cabins are tucked into the woods along Lake Huron, super-cozy, fireplaces and all. Reserve far in advance. I've eaten happily at Alpena's *Thunderbird Inn*.

On the other side of the state, *Point West*, between Lake Michigan and the west end of Lake Macatawa, easily fits on the roster of top resort-restaurants. Holland is the nearby city.

At Glen Arbor in the land of the Sleeping Bear, *The Homestead* offers accommodations in a woodsy, elegant setting, along with a grand view of the dunes. Two places outside of Harbor Springs should be mentioned: the *Harbour Inn*, a registered historic site, and the *Birchwood*, a lovely retreat on M-119.

Leg's Inn at Cross Village is almost an institution on to itself. One look at the bent-limb decor will tell you why ... plus come-again hamburgers.

At Mackinac Island the legendary *Grand Hotel* needs no comment, but I think the *Island House* is also very special. Actually, it's hard to go wrong on Mackinac.

St. Ignace's venerable antique, the *Colonial House*, is being lovingly restored and added to; the folks at *Straits Breeze* could hardly be friendlier.

On U.S. 2, Naubinway offers the *very* humble gas and eat stop, *Beaudoin's Cafe*, where the pie is great. On around the top of Lake Michigan try the *Fireside* in Manistique, the *Log Cabin* (for dinner) between Gladstone and Escanaba, or *Schloegels* in Menominee.

Eat hearty in Marquette. The *Onion Crock* in Marquette Mall is great for soup and carrot cake, and I like lunch at the *Depot* ... where you catch the steam train. (Hope it's still open.) At dinnertime, try the *Crow's Nest*, *Northwood Inn*, or *Tiroler Hof*.

Approaching Houghton, the modest-looking *Summer Place* restaurant is superb; the *Country House* in Kearsarge and *Harbor Haus* in Copper Harbor are run with a fine German culinary hand. To try that hearty marvel, the pasty (rhymes with nasty), the *Parkside* in Calumet is a good choice.

One of my most favorite places in the whole world is the Keweenaw Mountain Lodge, way up near Copper Harbor. Deluxe cabins in the woods, big comfortable lodge with excellent dining in a beautiful area.

One last word on this purely personal list: I also rather like the *Douglass House Hotel* in Houghton, a leftover from the old days with no delusions about past granduer. I find the old-but-clean, slightly threadbare hotel a refreshing change from the packaged sameness of the slick chains. Besides, the price is right.

FOR THE YOUNG AND THE RESTLESS

WHEN are we going to get there, Daddy?" The home driveway may be only two blocks behind when the questions start; part and parcel of traveling with kids. There's no cure, but a few game plans help. Every school-aged child in your car should have pencil, paper, and a map that doesn't have to be shared. Bring the kitchen minute-minder to call times.

—See how many words can be found in the letters M-I-C-H-I-G-A-N (or a county or city name).

—Choose a letter, then list places beginning with that letter. Extra points for places that begin and *end* with the letter.

—How many miles between Detroit and Algonac? South Haven and Ludington? The Soo and Paradise? Name your own combinations. (I.e., let *them* work out some trip details.)

—Put the letters of the alphabet on a piece of paper. At starting signal write down any object you drive past beginning with that letter. A ... auto, B ... barn, C ... cow, etc. To make it a little harder for the big kids, say that the word has to have at least five letters.

—Find out exactly where you are, name a town ahead, and guess how many minutes it will take to arrive. Repeat five times; person with most right guesses wins.

—Try to make the whackiest names you can with license plate

letters. Example: GWM—Geronimo Washington Mozart; KPS—Kitchen-pot Sally. Or find famous names in licenses: DD—Doris Day; GP—Gomer Pyle, General Patton, etc.

—Give each player a list of things to spot (and verify with one other person). A bank, a white barn, a house with a red roof, etc.

—Take turns dreaming up a mystery destination. Example: I'm thinking of a state park in a county beginning with "E" and a large bridge is not far away. Answer: Wilderness State Park in Emmet County, not far from Mackinac Bridge. Winner gets to think up the next one.

As every beleaguered parent knows, such diversion will only go so far, which is about two miles in some cases. Try a non-game called family conversation. (If you were going to build a new school, what would you put in it? Why do you suppose barns are so big? If you had to live in a totally different place, where would you go?) The miles can be eye-openers.

For some more travel games, send $1.00 to The Beavers, Star Route, P.O. Box 184, Laport, Minnesota 56461.

FAIRS AND FESTIVALS
AT A GLANCE

SINCE exact dates vary from year to year, I can only give you approximate times with no guarantees.

MAY •

Beginning of the month:
    Ethnic festivals featuring a different nationality group every weekend, May into September   Yack Arena—Wyandotte
        Hart Plaza—Detroit
    Blossomtime Festival—last of April, first of May   St. Joseph– Benton Harbor
Mid-month:
    Tulip Festival   Holland
    Mayfest—Muskegon Community College   Muskegon
Late in the month:
    Fort Michilimackinac Pageant—Memorial Day weekend   Mackinaw City

JUNE •

Early in the month:
    Frontier Days—Fort Wayne   Detroit
    Arts & Crafts Fair—Village Square Park   Saugatuck
    Lilac Festival   Mackinac Island
Mid-month:
    Asparagus Festival   Hart (near Pentwater)
    100-Meter Road Race   Cheboygan
    Vintage Auto Festival—White Pine Village   Ludington
    Historic Festival   Petoskey
    White Lake Arts & Crafts Festival   Whitehall
    Antique Auto Show/Flea Market— Fairgrounds   Bay City
Late in the month:
    Antique Auto Show—Dock #2   St. Ignace
    Thimbleberry Blossom Festival   Houghton
    Seaway Festival   Muskegon
    Fort Miami Day—Morton Museum   Benton Harbor

Early in the month:

Arts and Crafts Show	Drummond Island
Venetian Festival of Arts	Saugatuck
Lakeside Hobbycraft Show—East Park	Charlevoix
Fourth of July Sailboat Races	Alpena
Fourth of July Celebration	St. Ignace
National Forest Festival	Manistee
Western Amateur Golf Championship	St. Joseph–
	Benton Harbor
Washington Park Art Show	Cheboygan
Twin City Festival	Sault Ste. Marie
International Freedom Festival	Detroit/Windsor
National Soaring & Gliding Festival—	
Elberta Bluffs/Frankfort Airport	Elberta/Frankfort
National Cherry Festival	Traverse City
Heritage Week, White Pine Village	Ludington
Art & Craft Fair—Village Park	Pentwater
Outdoor Art Fair—Lake Bluff Park	St. Joseph
Strawberry Festival	Chassell

Mid-month:

National Blueberry Festival	South Haven
Street Art Fair—Biddle Avenue & Yack	
Arena	Wyandotte
Up in Central Park Art Fair	Grand Haven
International Frisbee Festival, exact site	
varies	Copper County
Thunder Bay Art Show—Mich-e-kewis Park	Alpena
Copper Country Art & Craft Show	Houghton
Floral City Festival	Monroe
Waterfront Festival	Harbor Beach
Sugar Festival	Sebewaing
Summer Festival	Bay City
King Salmon Derby Starts	Tawas
Paul Bunyan Festival	Oscoda
Annual Regatta	Tawas

Late in the month:

Arts & Crafts Shore—Bay Shore Park	Munising
Traverse Bay Outdoor Art Fair—	
Northwestern Michigan College	Traverse City

199

Art on the Rocks—Presque Isle Park	Marquette
Venetian Festival	Charlevoix
Venetian Festival	Saugatuck
Antique Show & Sale—Riverview Plaza	St. Clair
Old French Town Days—Community College	Monroe
Wanigan Week	Cheboygan
St. Clair County Fair	Port Huron
Ontonagon County Fair	Ontonagon
Venetian Festival	St. Joseph
Harbor Days	Elk Rapids

AUGUST •

Early in the month:

Waterfront Art Festival—Ludington Park	Escanaba
Waterfront Art Exhibit—City Park	Tawas City
Straits Area Arts & Crafts Show—Dock #2	St. Ignace
Water Festival—Riverfront	St. Clair
Monroe County Fair	Monroe
Nautical City Festival—Lakeside Park	Rogers City
Art Fair—East Park	Charlevoix
Antique Boat Show—Marina	Hessel
Art in the Park—Centennial Park	Holland
Indian Pow Wow	Cross Village
Highland Games—Township Hall	Gulliver
Summerfest	Drummond Island

*Early to Mid-*month:

Bay County Fair	Bay City
Arts Fest, Cheboygan to Bois Blanc Sail-in	Cheboygan
Rock Swap & Frisbee Competition	Marquette
Monroe County Fair	Monroe
Upper Peninsula State Fair	Escanaba

*Mid-*month:

Western Michigan Fair	Ludington
Art Fair—Pennsylvania Park	Petoskey
Arts & Crafts Fair—Village Square Park	Saugatuck

Late in the month:

Upper Peninsula State Fair	Escanaba
Summer Festival	Marine City
Michigan State Fair	Detroit
Northwestern Michigan Fair	Traverse City
Menominee County Fair	Menominee

American Salmon Derby	Ludington
Emmet County Fair	Petoskey
Schoolcraft County Fair	Manistique
Alpena County Fair	Alpena
Early in the month:	
Mackinac Bridge Walk—Labor Day	St. Ignace to Mackinaw City
Harvest Festival & Tri State Regatta—Labor Day Weekend	Benton Harbor– St. Joseph
All Craft Fair—Johnston Park	South Haven
Coho are running—Fishing Derbies everywhere	
Fence Art Sale & Show—Art Gallery	Tawas City
Black Gown Tree Pageant—Kiwanis Beach	St. Ignace
Upper Peninsula Steam & Gas Engine Show—Fairgrounds	Escanaba

● SEPTEMBER

This generally marks the closing of summer, but you might remember the Octoberfests (Sept.) in Copper Harbor, the Harvest Festival in the Lakeview Arena of Marquette, and the Indian Summer Festival at Saugatuck.

To get the total list of events, sports, theater, music, and special pageants along the coast and throughout the state, write to Travel Bureau, P.O. Box 30226, Lansing, Michigan 48909. Call toll-free: In state—800/292-2520; Out-of-state—800/248-5700 (CT, D.C., DE, IL, IN, IA, KY, MD, MN, MO, NJ, NY, OH, PA, TN, VT, VA, WV, WI).

WHAT IS A HARBOR OF REFUGE?

Not quite any port in a storm. In 1947 the Michigan State Waterways Commission launched an ambitious program to develop a chain of harbors and public marinas no more than thirty miles apart, so that when the winds blew and the waves rolled no boater would be more than fifteen miles from shoreline safety. New breakwaters and docks were built and existing facilities expanded until there are now sixty-five such designated harbors in public use.

Although basic harbor construction is paid by Federal and Michigan State funds, grants-in-aid have been given to local communities for the construction of extra facilities. The local folks then run the harbors, enforce the rules, and collect the fees for use as maintenence money.

All boaters seeking calmer waters in a storm may use the harbors; not all can dock whenever they wish, however. No matter what you've been told, there is no "right of the sea" automatically allowing you to tie up to a dock. The Waterways Commission's agreement with the local communities stipulates that a minimum of fifty percent of the boat wells are for the use of transients on a first-come, first-served basis; no advance registrations. Generally there is a seven-day limit on the time you can tie up to the same spot.

If you plan to buy fuel, have cash or be ready to pull out the credit card of the company named on the pump. Some harbors will let you add the dock fees to your fuel bill, others will not. These rules are often out of the hands of the local operators.

Observe the safety rules and the dock attendant's instructions when refueling as this can be a dangerous moment. The attendant, by the way, will probably be a college boy at a seasonal job and he is told to listen to your orders regarding docking. Ask for help if you need it.

Reminders to be courteous should hardly be necessary, but the boorish boaters of this world are slow to catch on. Reduce to a no-wake speed when you enter the harbor, go to the service booth first, then to a well. Noise on the water, after-dark parties, loud radios, and barking dogs . . . well, watch it. You may be asked to pull out.

Fees: These are set by the Waterways Commission and are standard (with rare exceptions such as Mackinac Island). As of the 1981 season, rates were as follows:

Boats less than 20 feet	$3.75
20 and over, less than 30 feet	$ .28 per foot
30 and over, less than 40 feet	$ .29 per foot
40 and over, less than 50 feet	$ .30 per foot
50 and over, less than 54 feet	$ .31 per foot

STATE PARKS OF THE LONG BLUE EDGE

LAKE ERIE, LAKE HURON		Acres	No. of Camp- sites
Sterling State Park	Lake Erie; Monroe I-75	997	192
Algonac	St. Clair River, Algonac M-29	1,023	300
Lakeport	Port Huron M-25	565	256
Sanilac	Forestville M-25	112	19
Port Crescent	Port Austin M-25	655	181
Sleeper	Caseville M-25	1,003	271
Bay City	Bay City M-247	196	255
Tawas Point	East Tawas U.S. 23	175	202
Harrisville	Harrisville U.S. 23	94	229
Hoeft	Rogers City U.S. 23	301	144
Cheboygan	Cheboygan U.S. 23	932	78
Michilimackinac	Mackinaw City I-75	No camping etc.	
Aloha	Cheboygan M-212	91	284
Straits (U.P.)	St. Ignace I-75	181	318
DeTour (U.P.)	St. Ignace M-134	403	22
LAKE MICHIGAN			
Warren Dunes	Sawyer I-94	1,502	197
Van Buren	South Haven I-196	326	205
Holland	Holland U.S. 31	143	342
Grand Haven	Grand Haven U.S. 31	48	170
Hoffmaster	Muskegon U.S. 31	1,043	333
Muskegon	North Muskegon M-213	1,125	357
Silver Lake	Mears U.S. 31	2,635	249

Mears	Pentwater U.S. 31	50	179
Ludington	Ludington M-116	4,156	398
Orchard Beach	Manistee M-110	201	175
Leelanau	Northport M-201	1,044	42
Interlochen	Interlochen M-137	187	550
Traverse City	Traverse City U.S. 31	39	330
Petoskey	Petoskey U.S. 31	305	90
Wilderness	Carp Lake U.S. 31	7,514	210
Indian Lake (U.P.)	Manistique U.S. 2	567	300
Palms Brook (U.P.)	Manistique U.S. 2	308	No camping
Fayette (U.P.)	Garden Co. Rd. 483	365	80
Wells (U.P.)	Cedar River M-35	974	155
LAKE SUPERIOR			
Brimley	Brimley M-221	151	270
Tahquamenon Falls	Paradise M-123	21,241	319
Muskallonge Lake	Newberry M-123	217	179
Van Riper	Champion U.S. 41	1,044	226
Baraga	Baraga U.S. 41	56	137
Fort Wilkins	Copper Harbor U.S. 41	199	165
McLain	Hancock M-203	401	90
Porcupine Mts.	Ontonagon M-107	58,332	199

POACHERS ARE STEALING

The Department of Natural Resources has a new program aimed at stopping the poaching of fish and game. Entitled "Report all Poaching" (RAP), there is a toll-free 24-hour hotline for the public to call when they have information on fish or game violations. A rewards system for such information resulting in the arrest and prosecution of poachers is part of the program.

If you spot off-season hunters, fishermen, etc., call 1-800/292-7800. Don't play policeman and try to detain someone yourself. You could get deep into legal hot water . . . or personal danger.

FEES AND REGULATIONS (as of Summer 1982)

CAMPING RESERVATION HOW TO'S: Some 6,000 of the camping • STATE PARKS spaces at sixty-three state parks are open to reservations covering the May-September 30 period. The remaining more than 7,000 campsites at parks are available on a first come, first-served basis. Application blanks for reservations and brochures explaining the system are available at all state parks, DNR regional and district offices, and travel offices. They also may be obtained from the DNR's Parks Division, P.O. Box 30028, Lansing, Michigan 48909.

RULES FOR YOUR CAMPING PLEASURE: To make your stay as pleasant as possible and to be fair to others, these rules have been adopted for all state park campgrounds:

1. Camping is permitted in established camping areas.
2. Not more than one camp, occupied by a single family or group, will be permitted on an individual site. No camp shall occupy more than one site. It must be occupied during the first twenty-four hour period.
3. Between June 15 and Labor Day, a permit will be revoked for any camp which is continuously left vacant for longer than twenty-four hours.
4. Quiet hours are from 11:00 PM to 7:00 PM

5. Fires are permitted only in stoves, grills, or designated fire circles.

6. Dogs must be kept under immediate control on a leash not exceeding six feet. They must not be left unattended. Dogs are not allowed on bathing beaches.

STATE FORESTS ● *FEE*: To keep our program operating, a $3.00 camping fee per camp per day will be assessed at all state forest campgrounds year-round.

YOU MAY—

Stay up to fifteen days.

Camp only in designated sites.

Build a fire in a designated place.

Operate an ORV in the campground for entrance and departure *only*.

Keep a dog only if on a leash less than six feet in length.

YOU MAY NOT—

Leave your camp unoccupied for more than twenty-four hours.

Occupy more than one campsite.

Discharge firearms or air guns.

Possess or use fireworks.

Ride or keep a horse.

Be excessively noisy.

YOU CAN HELP INCREASE program efficiency and reduce state costs by:

1. Pay the camping fee.
2. Carry out as much of your trash as possible.
3. Leave the campsite in a clean condition.
4. Report any vandalism to the nearest DNR office or official.

Your cooperation and generosity will help keep the forest campground operating. Thank you for your help.

FOREST MANAGEMENT DIVISION
BOX 30028 LANSING, MICHIGAN 48909 (517/373-1275)

FISHING LICENSE FEES*

Resident Annual (also covers spouse; good for all species EX-
CEPT trout and salmon) .... $ 7.25

Senior (age 65 or older) Resident Annual (also covers spouse
and the blind; good for all species INCLUDING trout and
salmon) .... $ 1.00

Non-Resident Annual (does not cover spouse; good for all
species EXCEPT trout, salmon) $15.25

Non-Resident Husband-Wife (good for all species EXCEPT trout
and salmon) $20.25

Daily (covers both residents and non-residents but not their
spouses; good for all species INCLUDING trout and salmon.
License is valid only until **midnight** of date shown).   Per Day $ 3.75

Trout-Salmon (required for ALL persons to fish for trout and
salmon. EXCEPTIONS: not required for holders of Senior
licenses or their spouses; not required for holders of Daily
licenses) .... $ 7.25

*Fishing license required of all who have passed their 17th birthday.
For licenses which cover spouse, the spouse (wife or husband) must
have filled-out license in possession.

I have laid business aside
and gone a-fishing.
—Izaak Walton,
The Compleat Angler, 1653

Doubt not that angling will
prove so pleasant that it, like
virtue, will be reward unto
itself.
—Izaak Walton,
The Compleat Angler, 1653

PUBLIC HEALTH ADVISORY

Fish from certain locations may contain hazardous levels of environmental contaminants (listed in parentheses). Accordingly, the Michigan
Department of Public Health advises against eating any fish from:

*Pine River downstream from St. Louis (PBB); Chippewa River down-
stream from Chippewa Rd. (Isabella County), PBB; Saginaw River
(PBB, TCDD).

*South Branch Shiawassee River (M-59 to Owosso), Kalamazoo River
(Kalamazoo to Saugatuck), and Portage Creek (from Milham Park
to mouth, Kalamazoo county) PCB.

Tittabawasee River from Midland downstream (PBB, TCDD).

The Public Health Department further advises children, women who
expect to bear children, pregnant women and nursing mothers against
eating any fish as listed below, and advises all others to consume no
more than one meal (½ pound) per week of such fish:

*Lake trout from L. Michigan (PCB, DDT), L. Superior (PCB, DDT,
Mercury);

*Salmon from L. Michigan and tributaries (PCB, Mercury), L. Huron
and tributaries (PCB);

*Steelhead from L. Michigan and tributaries (PCB);
*Largemouth and smallmouth bass from L. St. Clair (Mercury);
*Catfish and carp from Saginaw Bay, L. St. Clair, L. Erie, and Detroit
  and St. Clair Rivers (PCB);
*Walleye, white bass, muskellunge, sheepshead from L. St. Clair, L.
  Erie, L. Huron south of Port Sanilac and Detroit and St. Clair Rivers
  (Mercury).

From *Michigan Fishing Guide,* '81-'82

FOR THAT PRIZE CATCH:

Master Angler Certificates are awarded fishermen who catch state-record fish, or one of the top 5 fish of their kind entered during the year. Arm patches are given all entrants whose fish meet established minimum size. To be eligible, fish must be weighed on certified scales, signatures of two witnesses obtained, and pictures taken (in color, with fisherman holding fish in side view, preferred). For details and entry forms, contact DNR offices. Deadline for entries is Jan. 10 of each year.

Species	Lbs. & Ozs.		
Lake Sturgeon	193 lbs.	Splake	16-4
Great Lakes Muskie	62-8	Brook Trout	6-2
Carp	61-8	Black Crappie	4-2
Lake Trout	53-0	Yellow Perch	3-12
Channel Catfish	47-8	Sauger	6-9
Flathead Catfish	38-2	Rock Bass	3-10
Chinook Salmon	46-1	Bluegill (Pumpkinseed)	2-10
Northern Pike	39-0	White Bass	2-11
Coho Salmon	30-9	Atlantic Salmon	22-1
Brown Trout	31-8	Kokanee Salmon	1-15½
Rainbow Trout (Steelhead)	26-8	Lake Whitefish	12-14
Sheepshead	26-0	Tiger Muskie (Hybrid)	51-3
Walleye	17-3	Northern Muskie	40-15
Largemouth Bass	11-15	Pink Salmon	3-½
Smallmouth Bass	9-4	Tiger Trout	9-4

1980; Check with DNR for updated list

FOR REEL RESULTS

Toll-free Telephone Fishing Hotline will help you decide where to try your luck.

From: Michigan cities outside of Lansing, phone 1-800/292-2520

From: Ohio, Indiana, Illinois, Wisconsin, Pennsylvania, Vermont, New York, New Jersey, Connecticut, Delaware, Maryland, Virginia, Washington, D.C., Kentucky, Tennessee, West Virginia, Missouri, Iowa, and Minnesota, phone 1-800/248-5703

The information you'll receive is based on weekly field reports from the Department of Natural Resources and input from district biologists, marina operators, etc.

Angling may be said to be so like mathematics that it can never be fully learnt.
—Izaak Walton,
The Compleat Angler, 1653

WATER WISDOM

It's not smart to fish out on the big lake in a small boat. Recommended minimum size is an eighteen-footer, with a wide beam and high freeboard.

—an approved life-saving device for every passenger
—combination green and red bow lights and a white stern light for night use
—an approved fire extinguisher (1¼-gal. foam, 4 lb. carbon dioxide, or 2 lb. dry chemical)
—a hand, mouth, or power whistle or horn audible for ½ mile.

- **THE LAW REQUIRES**

—a hand-operated bilge pump or pail
—a second motor or oars or paddles
—distress flares, flashlights
—a good compass and charts
—first aid kit
—suitable anchor and enough line to go down seven times the water depth.

- **COMMON SENSE WOULD ADD**

Rights of way:
    Meeting: Passing port-to-port is the rule
    Crossing: When in doubt, always yield
    Overtaking: You may pass on either side but the boat being passed always has the right-of-way and should hold its course and speed

- **KNOW THE RULES**

Sailboats: They always have the right-of-way over private power boats,
except when they are overtaking a boat or have switched from
sail to power themselves
Learn where your danger zones are and what to do to avoid collisions
before you start out.

STORM WARNINGS

Small craft warning (38 mph wind) Day = red triangle pennant
Night = red light over white light

Gale warnings (wind up to 54 mph) Day = two red pennants
Night = white light over red light

Whole gale warning (winds to 72 mph)
Day = red flag with black center
Night = two red lights

Hurricane (wind over 72 mph)
Day = two red flags with black centers
Night = white light between two red lights

For a small but life-saving fee, the Superintendant of Documents, Washington, D.C., 20402, will send you a copy of the *Recreational Boating Guide.* Everything you ought to know and then some.

The Coast Guard Auxiliaries offer courses in pleasure boating, knowing the buoy lights, currents, weather, marine laws, etc., during winter months. Consult your phone book for closest Coast Guard number and information on courses near you. In Detroit area call 226-6930 weekdays, 9:00-5:00.

Or call 800/243-6000 for U.S. Power Squadrons courses with trained instructions, teaching aids, etc.

MEET THE BUOYS

CAN • *Black,* odd-numbered. Cans mark *left* side of channel when returning from sea or lake.

NUN • *Red,* even-numbered. Nuns mark *right* side of channel when returning from sea.

SPAR • Black, red, or striped. Not numbered. *Horizontal* stripes means pass wide either side; vertical stripes mark mid-channel.

LIGHTED • *Red* light—keep right when returning from seaward; *green* light—keep
BUOY turning left when returning. White light can mark either side of channel.

WATERSKIING SAFETY

From the United States Coast Guard *Recreational Boating Guide*

1. Allow no one to ski who can't swim *well*. The ski belt is only to keep unconscious skiers afloat.

2. Water ski only in safe area, out of channels, away from other craft. Some lakes, etc. have areas designated for skiing plus places where skiing is forbidden.

3. Install wide-angle rearview mirror or take a second person to act as lookout.

4. Make sure skier is wearing life jacket.

5. If skier falls, approach from lee (the direction toward which the wind blows) side; stop motor *before* you start to take him aboard.

6. In taking the skier on board, be careful not to swamp the boat. Usually safest to take person aboard at the stern.

The American Water Ski Association has recommended that the following set of signals be known and understood by operator, skier, and observer:

Faster—palm of one hand pointing upward.
Slower—palm of one hand pointing downward.
Speed OK—arm raised, thumb and forefinger forming a circle.
Turn right—arm outstretched pointing right.
Turn left—arm outstretched pointing left.
Return to drop-off area—arms at 45° angle pointing down to water, swinging.
Cut motor—finger drawn across throat.
Stop—hand up, palm forward (traffic cop style).
Skier OK after fall—hands clenched overhead.
Pick me up or *Fallen skier–watch out*—one ski vertical out of water.

RULES OF THE MICHIGAN ROAD

SPEED LIMITS • The *maximum* speed any vehicle may travel on Michigan highways or freeways is *55 miles per hour*. On freeways, the minimum speed is 45 miles per hour.

In *business*, *residential*, and *park* areas where no speeds are posted, do not drive faster than *25 miles per hour*.

In *road construction* or *maintenance areas*, the speed limit is *45 miles per hour*.

RIGHT-OF-WAY • You must yield the right-of-way to ambulances and fire or police vehicles sounding a siren and flashing warning lights. Pull over to the right edge of the roadway clear of intersections and stop.

You must also yield the right-of-way to cars in a funeral procession and to traffic and pedestrians in an intersection.

LANE USAGE • You *must* drive in the right-hand lane in Michigan, except: 1) when passing slower vehicles, 2) when getting ready to make a left turn, or 3) when traveling on a one-way street in heavy traffic. However, you may drive in any lane of a freeway having three lanes in the same direction.

DRINKING AND DRIVING • Michigan (and every other state) has an *Implied Consent Law*. Under this law, any person who drives a motor vehicle on a public highway is considered to have given his consent to be tested to find out the alcoholic content of his blood.

ARREST AND BOND PROCEDURE • Answer the citation by *registered mail* or *in person* within the designated time limit, or forfeit your bond. Should you ever again be arrested in Michigan, you could be jailed until the earlier citation is resolved.

STOPPING FOR SCHOOL BUSES • Traffic in both directions must stop at least ten feet from a stopped school bus that has its red lights flashing. You must not pass the bus until the lights are turned off or the bus starts. On *divided* highways with an uncrossable median, traffic coming toward a school bus stopped on the other side of the road does not stop.

TURNING ON RED • Unless there is a sign telling you not to turn, you may:

1) turn right on a red light.

2) turn left on a red light when entering one-way streets where traffic is moving to the left. You always must come to a complete stop, then turn carefully.

At some intersections, a *steady green arrow* means you may turn carefully without stopping in the direction shown by the arrow; but, you must yield to pedestrians.

Use the entrance ramp and the acceleration lane to speed up until ● FREEWAY DRIVING you are going about as fast as freeway traffic. Watch out for cars directly ahead of you in the acceleration lane that may have slowed or stopped. Signal, look for an opening in traffic, and move into the travel lane.

Do not stop in an acceleration lane unless traffic is too heavy and there is no space for you to enter safely.

Never turn around or back up on a freeway. If you miss your exit, drive on and use the next exit.

Walking or hitchhiking on Michigan freeways and their entrance ● HITCHHIKING and exit ramps is *dangerous and against the law*. Do not stop to pick up hitchhikers on a freeway.

For a complete explanation of Michigan's traffic laws, ask the Department of State for a copy of "What Every Driver Must Know."

Thanks to Michigan Traffic Safety Information Council

AIDS FOR THE HANDICAPPED

The Michigan Travel Commission has prepared a *Handicapper's Mini-Guide* listing facilities and giving suggestions to persons who need wider doors, ramps, etc. Accommodations and popular attractions are listed as well as addresses for additional helpful information. For your copy, write: Michigan Travel Commission, P.O. Box 30226, Lansing, Michigan 48909.

MICHIGAN STATE POLICE POSTS

(Coastal cities only)

	area code	telephone
Detroit Area		
Detroit	313	256-9636
St. Clair	313	329-2233
New Baltimore	313	725-7503
Flat Rock	313	782-2434
East Michigan		
Bay City	517	684-2234
Bad Axe	517	269-6441
East Tawas	517	362-3434
Sandusky	313	648-2233
South Michigan		
Erie	313	848-2015
New Buffalo	616	469-1111
West Michigan		
South Haven	616	637-2125
Saugatuck	616	857-2800
Benton Harbor	616	926-7361
Grand Haven	616	842-2100
Hart	616	873-2171

North Michigan		
Traverse City	616	946-4646
Kalkaska	616	258-2831
Cheboygan	616	627-9973
Alpena	517	354-4101
Manistee	616	723-3535
Petoskey	616	347-8101
Upper Peninsula		
Negaunee (Marquette area)	906	475-9922
Newberry	906	293-5151
St. Ignace	906	643-8383
Manistique	906	341-2101
Gladstone	906	428-1212
L'Anse	906	524-6161
Stephenson (Menominee area)	906	753-2275
Calumet	906	337-2211
Munising	906	387-4550
Sault Ste. Marie	906	632-2216

Dept. Headquarters: So. Harrison Rd., East Lansing, 517/332-2521.

WHERE TO GET MORE INFORMATION

THE FRUIT SCOOP • For a guide to pick-your-own farms and roadside markets, write Communications Office, Michigan Department of Agriculture, P.O. Box 30017, Lansing, Michigan 48909.

FOR BIKERS • A free biking brochure is yours by writing to Michigan Bicycle Tours, 162 Golfview Drive, Brooklyn, Michigan 49230.

OFFICIAL FISHING GUIDE • Available free from Michigan Department of Natural Resources, S. T. Mason Bldg., Lansing, Michigan 48909. 517/373-1280. Contains all you need to know about licenses, seasons, special waters, size and creel limits, definitions, and field offices.

A map of each of Michigan's eighty-three counties included in a guide put out by the Michigan United Conservation Clubs. Write to: M.U.C.C., P.O. Box 30235, Lansing, Michigan 48909. Ask for the *Guide To Fun in Michigan;* $7.00 postpaid.
• DETAILED COUNTY MAPS

P.O. Box 30226, Lansing, Michigan 48909. Call toll free (in Michigan): 1-800/292-2520, or (out-of-state) 1-800/248-5700.
• TRAVEL BUREAU DEPARTMENT OF COMMERCE

64 Park Street, P.O. Box 1590, Troy, Michigan 48099-1590. 313/585-8220. Or phone 313/585-7233 for Travel Line tips on events, festivals, and special travel news in Southeast Michigan.
• TRAVEL AND TOURIST ASSOCIATION OF SOUTHEAST MICHIGAN

Log Office, One Wenonah Park, Bay City, Michigan 48706. 517/895-8823; within 517 area code, call toll-free 1-800/322-4825.
• EAST MICHIGAN TOURIST ASSOCIATION

136 East Fulton, Grand Rapids, Michigan 49503. 616/456-8557.
• WEST MICHIGAN TOURIST ASSOCIATION

P.O. Box 400, Iron Mountain, Michigan 49801. 906/774-5480.
• UPPER PENINSULA TRAVEL and RECREATION ASSOCIATION

For map information, inter-city bus and rail data, call district offices. (Not for general tourist aid, however.) Headquarters in Lansing Transportation Building, 517/373-2090.
• MICHIGAN DEPARTMENT OF TRANSPORTATION

Crystal Falls 906/875-6644	Jackson 517/784-7172
Newberry 906/293-5168	Saginaw 517/754-7443
Cadillac 616/775-3487	Kalamazoo (Portage) 616/
Alpena 517/356-2231	327-3054
Grand Rapids ...616/451-3091	Detroit Metropolitan 313/
	569-3993

Fisheries Division, Lansing .... (517) 373-1280
Fishing Conditions .... (517) 373-0908
Violations .... 1-(800) 292-7800
Information Services Center .... (517) 373-1220
• DEPARTMENT OF NATURAL RESOURCES OFFICES

UPPER PENINSULA

Marquette	(906) 226-7505
Baraga	(906) 353-6651
Crystal Falls	(906) 875-6622
Escanaba	(906) 786-2351
Newberry	(906) 293-5131

NORTHERN LOWER PENINSULA

Roscommon	(517) 275-5151
Gaylord	(517) 732-3541
Cadillac	(616) 775-9727
Mio	(517) 826-3211
Clare	(517) 386-7991

SOUTHERN LOWER PENINSULA

Lansing	(517) 322-1300
Grand Rapids	(616) 456-5071
Imlay City	(313) 724-2015
Plainwell	(616) 685-6851
Jackson	(517) 784-3188

SOURCES AND SUGGESTED READING

Atlas of Michigan—Michigan State University/Eerdmans Publishing Co.

Michigan: A History of the Wolverine State—Willis Dunbar, newly revised by George May, Eerdmans Publishing Co.

Michigan in Four Centuries—F. C. Bald, Harper and Row.

The Fate of the Lakes—James P. Barry, Bonanza Books.

The Enduring Great Lakes—Edited by John Rousmaniere, Norton Press.

Michigan—Bruce Catton, Norton.

A Pictorial History of the Great Lakes—Harlan Hatcher and Erich A. Walter, Bonanza Books.

Guardians of the Eighth Sea—United States Coast Guard Publication.

Mighty Mac: Picture History of Mackinac Bridge—Lawrence A. Rubin, published by Kiwanis Club of St. Ignace.

Mackinac Island: Its History in Pictures—Eugene T. Peterson, published by Mackinac Island State Park Commission.

Michigan—M. M. Quaife and Sidney Glazer, Prentice-Hall Inc.

Great Lakes Shipwrecks and Survivals—William Ratigan, Eerdmans Publishing Co.

Great Lakes Guidebooks—George Cantor, University of Michigan Press.

Geology of Michigan—John Dorr and Donald Eschman, University of Michigan Press.

Boom Copper—Angus Murdoch, Copper Country Publication.

Red Metal—C. Harry Benedict, University of Michigan Press.

Great Lakes Reader—Walter Havighurst, Collier Books.

Mackinac Island—Mary Duffina Summerfield, The Voyager, People & Places, Great Lakes Gazette, Inc.

Plus hundreds of brochures, area guides, tourist association publications, local newspapers, and a lifetime of Michigan living.

For your convenience, we've provided the next few pages for you to record information about your trip: the itinerary, mileage and expenses, your favorite places to visit, etc. Or, you may prefer to tear these pages out as you need them to write home! Enjoy your adventure on THE LONG BLUE EDGE OF SUMMER!

_____

_____

_____

_____

_____

_____

_____

_____

_____

_____

_____

_____

_____

_____

_____

_____

_____

_____

_____

_____

_____

_____

_____